Memory Mastery For Entrepreneurs

Simple Hacks To Boost Recall, Sharpen Focus, and Accelerate Success

Jeff Kikel

CPTX Media LLC

Publisher:
CPTX Media
1320 Arrow Point Dr, Ste 501
Cedar Park, TX 78613
www.cptxmedia.com

Cover Design: Khatoon Bibi

This publication is designed to provide accurate and authoritative information in regard to the subject matter covered. It is sold with the understanding that the author and publisher are not engaged in rendering legal, accounting, or other professional services. If legal advice or other expert assistance is required, the services of a competent professional should be sought.

Printed in the United States of America

First Edition: May 2025

Contents

Get Your Free Gift: The Memory Mastery Workbook + 10-Day Mini-Course!

Before you dive in, I've got a special gift for you.

As a thank-you for picking up Memory Mastery for Entrepreneurs, I've created a free downloadable workbook packed with:

Practical exercises from every chapter

Cheat sheets and templates to use right away

A personal memory dashboard to track your progress

PLUS: You'll get access to my brand-new Memory Mastery Mini-Course — delivered straight to your inbox over 10 days.

This mini-course will help you:

- Lock in the key strategies from this book
- Build daily habits without overwhelm
- Apply memory tools to real business challenges
- Boost your brainpower in under 10 minutes a day

It's like having me as your personal memory coach — guiding you step by step.

Grab your free workbook + mini-course here:

https://businessgrowthproject.co/memory-workbook708420

(And yes — it's 100% free. No strings attached. Just great tools to help you win the mental game of entrepreneurship.)

Let's make this your sharpest, most focused year yet!

— Jeff

Introduction: Why This Book, Why Now

If you're anything like me, your brain probably feels like a web browser with 47 open tabs — and at least three are frozen.

You've got names to remember, projects to juggle, client details floating around, big ideas hitting you in the shower, and somewhere in there, you're also trying to remember if you actually sent that email you drafted at 6 a.m. Oh, and let's not forget when you walk into a room and immediately ask yourself, *"Why did I come in here again?"*

Here's the honest truth: I didn't set out to become a "memory guy."

Like many of you, for most of my life, I walked around thinking I had a *pretty good* memory. I could remember faces, conversations, and random trivia from years ago — you know, the kind of facts that win you a few points on trivia night but don't exactly change your life. But when it came to names? Total disaster.

I was the king of "Hey, buddy!" or "How's it going, brother?" and my personal favorite, the head nod with a confident *"Good to see you!"* just to cover up the fact that I was blanking... again.

For a long time, I told myself it didn't really matter. But over time, it became clear that it did. It mattered when I missed out on deepening a client relationship because I couldn't remember the details we discussed. It mattered when I lost momentum on a big idea because I didn't capture it or follow up. And it mattered when I found myself running a growing business — or three — and realizing my brain wasn't quite keeping pace with my ambition.

That's when I realized this wasn't just a cute quirk. It was a gap that needed closing.

My Curiosity (and Embarrassment) Became My Mission

Like a lot of entrepreneurs, I'm naturally curious. So when I hit this wall, I did what I always do — I dove in.

I started digging into memory improvement, thinking I'd pick up a few party tricks and maybe remember people's names better. But what I discovered was so much bigger: I found tools and techniques that could sharpen my focus, boost my productivity, help me retain key learning, and even manage the mental chaos of running multiple businesses.

This book is the culmination of that journey. It's the playbook I wish I'd had 10 years ago—practical, actionable, and built for people like you and me who are spinning a lot of plates and want our brains to work *for* us, not against us. It's not just a collection of theories, but a set of tools you can start using today to improve your memory and productivity.

Why Entrepreneurs and Business Owners Need This

Look, memory isn't just about remembering where you left your keys or whether you added eggs to the grocery list (although that's certainly a nice side benefit).

It's about:

1. Remembering client names, details, and needs so you build trust and loyalty.

2. Retaining new skills and knowledge so you can keep evolving in your industry.

3. Capturing and organizing ideas so you can act on them when it matters.

4. Reducing mental clutter so you have the focus and space to make better decisions.

5. Protecting your most valuable asset: your brain.

As business owners, entrepreneurs, and busy professionals, we often put all our energy into optimizing our businesses and forget to optimize *ourselves*. But here's the truth: your brain is the ultimate competitive advantage. When you sharpen your memory, you sharpen everything else — your leadership, creativity, resilience, relationships. This book isn't just about helping you remember more. It's about helping you become more-more focused, more capable, more resilient. It's about giving you the edge you need to succeed in today's fast-paced, competitive business world.

What You'll Get (and What You Won't)

Let me tell you what this book is **not**.

It's not an academic dissertation packed with dry, jargon-heavy neuroscience (though don't be surprised if you pick up a few cool brain facts to casually drop at your next dinner party).

It's not a collection of quick-fix hacks that promise you a photographic memory by Friday.

And it's definitely not a lecture from some memory wizard claiming you should memorize 5,000 digits of pi just for fun.

What you **will** get is:

1. Simple, actionable strategies that work in real life.

2. Relatable stories (including a few embarrassing ones from yours truly) that show you how these tools fit into daily life.

3. Practical exercises at the end of each chapter that give you quick wins.

Expect a conversational, lighthearted tone throughout the book — because learning works better when we're enjoying ourselves. This is not a dry, academic read, but a friendly guide for your busy brain.This is a **field guide for busy brains** — written by someone who knows exactly what it's like to juggle multiple roles, businesses, and priorities and still wants to be mentally sharp at the end of the day.

A Preview of What's Inside

In Chapter 1, you'll hear how my own memory wake-up call kicked off this journey. Spoiler: it involved years of awkwardly dodging people's names and finally realizing I couldn't keep skating by with charm alone.

We'll cover:

1. Why sleep, diet, and exercise are the foundation of every sharp mind.

2. How to structure your day for maximum focus and minimal overwhelm.
3. Tricks like mnemonics, the memory palace, and chunking that make memorization easier and even fun.
4. The power of habit tracking and how offloading routine decisions frees up your brain for the big stuff.
5. How to use digital tools wisely without turning your brain to mush.
6. Why managing stress isn't just good for your mood — it's critical for your memory.
7. And the secret sauce that holds it all together: review and repetition.

By the time you finish, you'll have a memory system you can use every day — without needing a PhD, a 90-minute morning routine, or a private coach.

Why This Book Now?

After 30 years in business, I've learned that the stakes have never been higher for entrepreneurs and leaders to stay sharp.

We're facing unprecedented levels of distraction. The world moves fast, and change happens faster. If you can't keep up mentally, you fall behind—or worse, you burn out.

But when you take control of your memory, everything changes.

1. You make smarter decisions because you remember key details.
2. You build stronger relationships because you remember names and conversations.
3. You innovate more easily because you remember and connect ideas across time.
4. You reduce stress because you have systems that help you manage complexity.

This book isn't just about helping you remember more. It's about helping you *become more* — more focused, more capable, more resilient.

My Promise to You

Here's what I want you to know before you turn the page:

You don't need to be a genius.

You don't need to have some special "memory gene."

You don't need to carve out three hours a day for brain training.

What you *do* need is curiosity, a willingness to practice, and the belief that you can improve — because you can.

This book will meet you wherever you are, whether you're an experienced entrepreneur or someone just getting started on your personal growth journey. My goal is to give you tools you can apply immediately, build momentum over time, and weave into your business and life without adding more overwhelm.

A Personal Invitation

I'm not here to preach at you from some mountaintop of mastery.

I'm in the trenches with you — running businesses, managing teams, raising a family, juggling life, and still figuring it out daily. I've seen firsthand how much easier (and more fun) business becomes when your brain works *for* you, not against you.

So, I invite you to join me on this journey. Bring your curiosity, skepticism, and sense of humor.

Together, we'll build a brain that's sharper, stronger, and ready for anything life throws your way.

One Last Thing Before We Dive In

This isn't about perfection.

It's about progress.

If you walk away from this book with even one or two tools that make you feel sharper, calmer, and more confident, then I consider that a win.

If you find yourself remembering a client's name without panic, recalling an idea when you need it, or simply feeling more in control of your mental game — that's success.

So, let's turn the page and get started.

Your brain — and your business — are about to thank you.

Chapter One

The Entrepreneur's Brain — Understanding Memory

Let me tell you a little secret.

I've got one of those quirky memories.

I can meet someone once, ten years ago, and remember what we talked about, where we were, what we drank — heck, even the wallpaper color in the room. But ask me their name? I'm toast.

That's why, for years, I became a master of the *strategic greeting.*

"Hey, man!"

"Good to see you, brother!"

"How's it going, you?"

It became my go-to at networking events, coffee meetups, and conferences. And for a while, it worked like magic. People smiled, shook my hand, and we carried on like old pals. But deep down, I knew — I was skating on thin ice.

There was this one moment — the tipping point — when I ran into a guy I'd met three times before. Three. Not once. Not twice. Three times. And I still blanked on his name. I leaned in with a **"How's it going, champ?"** and I could feel his eyebrows twitch just a little — like, *"Really, Jeff? Still?"*

That night, while driving home, I had a long, honest talk with myself (yes, I do talk to myself in the car). I realized that while my memory could handle details, stories, and faces, I was absolutely flunking the name game. And as any entrepreneur knows, relationships drive opportunities. You're missing half the game if you can't remember the person.

So, I went down the rabbit hole.

I read books. Took online courses. Watched TED talks. I even experimented with memory techniques on my own — like a lab rat testing out brain hacks. Some worked, some fizzled, and some were just plain weird (I'll tell you about the "name sandwich" experiment later — yeah, that's a thing).

This book is the cheat sheet I wish someone had handed me years ago. Not just dry theory, but what *actually works* — especially when you're running a business, juggling clients, staff, deadlines, and the twelve browser tabs open in your brain.

Why Memory Is Your Hidden Superpower

Here's something we rarely talk about as entrepreneurs:

Memory is **your silent competitive edge**.

You can have the fanciest software, the biggest email list, the slickest sales funnel... but if you can't remember conversations, connections, ideas, or the people you meet, you're leaving money — and relationships — on the table.

Think about it.

When you remember a client's name, their last big win, or even their kid's soccer game, it lands differently. It shows you care. It builds trust. And trust is where business happens.

Memory is what separates the good networker from the unforgettable one.

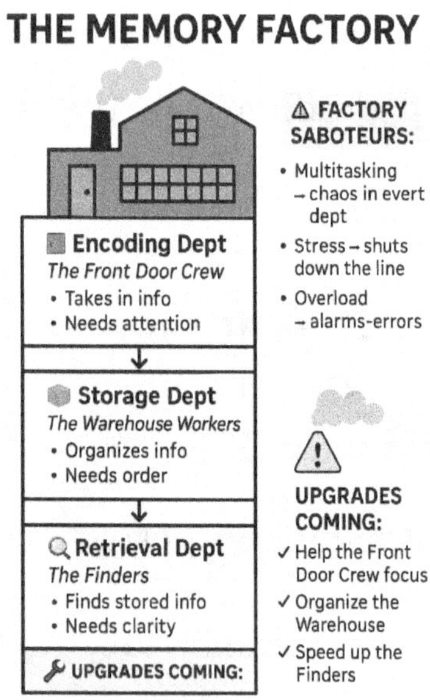

What's Happening In Your Brain (Without the Boring Lecture)

Okay, let's break it down like we're at happy hour, not in biology class.

Your brain has a system for managing information. Here's the cheat sheet:

1. **Encoding** → this is how your brain takes in

information. If you're half-listening, stressed, or distracted, encoding is weak. You can't remember what you never *noticed* in the first place.

2. **Storage** → This is where the information lives. If encoding is the bouncer at the club door, storage is the VIP room. Some stuff gets in, and some stuff doesn't.

3. **Retrieval** → This is when you reach back and say, *"What was her name again?"* If the memory was never encoded well, retrieval is like looking for your keys in a dark room. Good luck.

When people say, *"I have a terrible memory,"* they often mean one of these three steps isn't working well—and most of the time, it's because we're just **doing too much**.

Why Entrepreneurs Get Stuck

Let's be honest.

Entrepreneurs are a special breed of chaos. We're running meetings, launching campaigns, troubleshooting tech, answering emails, and putting out fires — often all before lunch. Our brains? They're like overworked warehouse workers trying to sort packages as fast as possible.

And then we wonder why we forget names, details, or even why we walked into the room.

Here's what messes us up:

1. **Multitasking** - Sorry, but humans are awful at it. The more you divide your attention, the worse your memory works.

2. **Stress** - Cortisol — your stress hormone — floods your brain and messes with memory retrieval.

3. **Information overload** - You get 50 Slack messages and 200 emails, and your brain finally just says, *"Nope. I'm out."*

Here's the good news: You can hack the system.

Your Memory Dream Team

Let's get to know the players:

1. **Short-term memory:** This is your brain's

sticky note. You can hold about seven bits of information at a time (ever wonder why license plates in the U.S. are 7 digits?). But if you don't transfer it to long-term memory, it's gone by tomorrow.

2. **Long-term memory:** This is your hard drive. It stores memories, skills, facts, and emotional experiences. You can fit a LOT in here, but you need a system to file it.

3. **Working memory:** This is your mental whiteboard. It lets you temporarily hold information while you process it, like remembering a client's order while you're writing up the invoice.

Most of us overload the sticky notes, scribble all over the whiteboard, and forget to back up to the hard drive. That's why we need better habits.

The Sneaky Power of Memory

Here's why this matters in business:

1. You remember the **details** others forget. ("Hey Mike, how was that big move last month?")

2. You follow through on promises. ("I'll email you that resource we talked about.")

3. You stand out in a sea of forgettable handshakes.

The best part? You don't need to be born with a "photographic memory." You just need to learn a few simple tools — which is exactly what's coming in the next chapters.

My "Name Recovery Mission"

Quick side story — once I started experimenting with memory techniques, I tried everything to fix my name problem.

I played with repeating people's names as soon as they introduced themselves.

I imagined their names written on their forehead.

I even tried the "name sandwich," where you say their name at the conversation's start, middle, and end. (Spoiler: that one made me sound like a chatbot.)

What worked?

It was a combination of attention (actually *listening* when they said their name), association (linking the name to something visual), and rehearsal (repeating it silently while we chatted).

And it didn't just help names — it sharpened how I paid attention to people, period.

Exercise: Your Memory Self-Check

Let's kick things off with a quick win.

Grab a notebook or your phone and answer these:

1. Do you naturally remember faces or names better?
2. Are you better at remembering numbers or stories?
3. When's a time your memory saved you in business?
4. When's a time your memory embarrassed you?

Write them down. No judgment.

This isn't a test — it's a starting point.

Next, over the next **three days**, pay attention to when you notice your memory *working* or *slipping*. Did you remember someone's name without looking them up? Did you forget why you walked into the room? Jot it down.

By simply noticing, you'll already start rewiring your brain to care.

A Quick Pep Talk

Listen, you're not broken.

You don't have a "bad brain" or "bad memory."

You just have an overloaded, under-trained system — and we're about to change that.

In the chapters ahead, we'll cover:

1. How lifestyle tweaks (sleep, food, stress) improve memory.
2. Simple hacks like mnemonics and visualization to lock in key info.
3. Tools and apps (like memoryOS, BrainHQ, and yes, even Lumosity) that make practice fun.
4. How to use your improved memory as a business advantage.

And don't worry — we'll keep it simple, fun, and real.

One Last Thing Before We Move On

Here's the truth: You're already better at memory than you realize.

Your brain is working hard behind the scenes — you just need to *help it help you.*

So be patient. Be curious. And remember (no pun intended) — you don't need perfection.

You just need progress.

If you're ready, I'll meet you in Chapter 2, where we clean up your sleep, your stress, and maybe even your snack drawer.

Trust me — your brain will thank you.

Final Exercise Checklist:

1. Answer the four memory reflection questions.
2. Track memory "wins" and "slips" over the next three days.
3. Pat yourself on the back — you're already ahead of most people just by paying atten-

tion.

Chapter Two

Building a Memory-Friendly Lifestyle

Do you know those airplane stories where someone sits next to a celebrity or a millionaire, and their life changes forever?

Well, that wasn't exactly me.

But on one memorable business trip, I *did* end up sitting next to someone pretty remarkable — a **sleep researcher and author**. And honestly, for a memory nerd like me, it might as well have been Bono or Oprah.

For three straight hours at 30,000 feet, we dove deep into one of my favorite topics: sleep, memory, and why most of us are running our brains into the ground.

That day, I learned something that changed how I think about my brain: **each of us has a unique sleep pattern that we need to respect.**

After that flight, I made a conscious decision to take charge of my health and well-being by experimenting with the most critical startup I've ever had: myself.

For weeks, I tracked my sleep. I tried going to bed earlier, sleeping in later, cutting caffeine, adding exercise, and even avoiding late-night emails (which, for an entrepreneur, is like asking a dog not to chase squirrels).

And here's what I discovered:

I'm a **6-to-7-hour guy.**

During the week, I can cruise on 6 hours, wake up at 5 a.m. without an alarm, and hit the ground running. But on weekends, if I oversleep past that window, I feel like I've got mental jet lag — groggy, sluggish, foggy.

That airplane chat didn't just make me sleep-obsessed; it woke me up to another truth: **my diet matters, too.**

Thankfully, my wife and I love to cook, and we avoid processed and fast food. When I eat clean, I notice I'm sharper, quicker, and way less reliant on my morning coffee to feel alive.

The punchline?

Your brain needs care. It's not about hacks or shortcuts — it's about fuel, rest, and respect.

Why Lifestyle Is the Foundation of Memory

Look, I love a good app or memory trick as much as anyone. But if you're running on four hours of sleep, washing it down with two energy drinks and a breakfast burrito, no app in the world is going to save you.

Memory isn't just a brain thing — it's a **whole-body thing.**

When you sleep, your brain cleans house.

Literally.

Throughout the day, you build up waste — metabolic junk — in your brain. While sleeping, your brain clears it out like a night shift cleaning crew. Skip sleep, and that waste piles up, clogging your ability to think, process, and remember.

And food?

Your brain runs on it.

Eat nutrient-rich, whole foods like leafy greens, fruits, and lean proteins, and your brain hums along like a well-oiled machine. Avoid sugar, fried junk, and processed food like donuts, chips, and fast food, and your brain feels like it's trying to sprint through molasses.

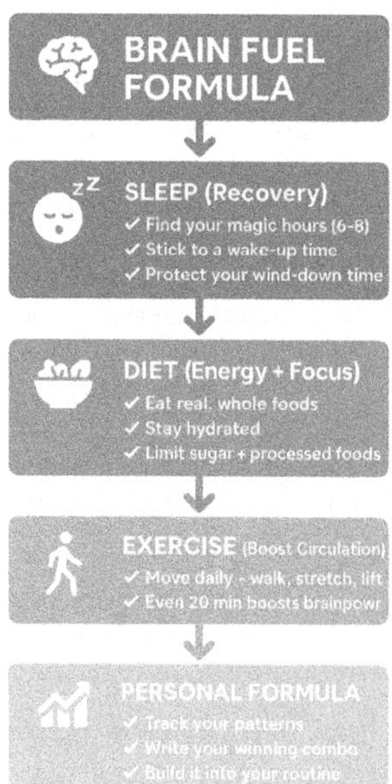

When you fuel your brain, you fire up your business

Finding *Your* Sweet Spot

Here's the key: **Everyone's formula is different.**

Some folks need 8 hours.

Others thrive on 6 or 7.

A few unicorns run on 5 — but they're rare (and probably lying).

The point is you need to experiment. You wouldn't copy someone else's business plan without adapting it to your market, right? The same goes for your brain.

For me, 6–7 hours is the magic zone.

For you, it might be different.

And trust me — it's worth figuring out.

Sleep Tactics That Actually Work

Let me save you some time (and failed experiments).

Here's what works for most people:

1. **Track your sleep** for a week or two. No fancy gadget is required — jot down what time you go to bed, wake up, and how you feel.

2. **Find your personal sleep window.** Notice when you feel the sharpest. Is it after 6, 7, or 8 hours?

3. **Stick to a regular wake-up time.** Your brain *loves* consistency, even on weekends.

4. **Avoid the 'sleep-in hangover,' a term used to describe the grogginess and disorientation that can result from sleeping longer than your body needs.** Sleeping 10 hours on Sunday doesn't make up for the 4 you got on Friday. In fact, it can leave you foggy and less alert.

5. **Create a wind-down routine.** This could include activities like reading a book, taking a warm bath, or practicing relaxation techniques. Avoid bingeing on Netflix or doomscrolling social media right before bed, as these activities can overstimulate your brain and make it harder to fall asleep. If you're wondering whether your phone in bed is wrecking your brain, the answer is yes. And no, switching to "night mode" doesn't fix it.

The Power of the Power Nap

Later in my memory journey, I discovered a little secret: you don't have to get all your brain fuel in one overnight shot.

Enter one of the entrepreneur's best-kept productivity tools: **the 10–15 minute power nap.**

I know, I know — you're busy, you don't have time to snooze like a cat on the couch. But hear me out.

Research shows that even a short nap—as little as **10 to 20 minutes**—can dramatically improve memory, focus, creativity, and decision-making. We're not talking about a two-hour Saturday afternoon nap that leaves you groggy and stumbling into the kitchen. This is a *purposeful reset*.

Here's how it works:

1. A short nap helps your brain consolidate information you've recently taken in.
2. It clears mental fatigue, so you can tackle the afternoon with sharper focus.
3. It's long enough to refresh but short enough to

avoid dropping into deep sleep (which can leave you foggy).

I personally use power naps as a mental **"reset button"** on heavy days — and yes, sometimes they happen in the car (yes, I am parked), sometimes in my office chair, and once or twice, I've been caught by my cat snoozing on the living room floor.

The key?

1. Set a timer for 15–20 minutes.
2. Keep it short — this isn't about REM sleep. It's about a mental pit stop.
3. Don't feel guilty. You're not being lazy — you're investing in your brain.

So, alongside finding your "magic" sleep hours at night, consider sprinkling in a power nap when your brain hits that predictable afternoon dip. You might be surprised how much clearer, calmer, and sharper you feel.

Feeding Your Brain

Now, about that diet.

I'm not here to turn you into a kale evangelist or tell you to quit carbs forever. But here's the truth:

Your brain is about 2% of your body weight...

and it uses about 20% of your energy.

That's a massive fuel requirement.

And it's why what you eat matters so much.

Here's what works for me (and what science backs up):

1. **Eat real food.** More veggies, fruits, lean proteins, healthy fats. Less packaged junk.

2. **Stay hydrated.** Dehydration shrinks your brain tissue — literally. Drink water, not just coffee.

3. **Watch the sugar.** A sugar crash will wipe out your focus and your mood.

4. **Cook at home when you can.** Not only does it boost nutrition, but it's also good for your relationships — and for your wallet.

Fast food may be fast, but it makes your brain feel like it's running on dial-up. Remember dial-up? Exactly.

Exercise: The Bonus Brain Booster

You don't need to become a gym rat.

But even a 20-minute walk, some light weights, or a yoga session improves blood flow, oxygen, and memory function. Movement matters — and it's the simplest upgrade you can give your brain.

A few years ago, I decided to develop an exercise habit that I have continued consistently for 782 days in a row. I decided to commit to two exercises per night, including kettlebell exercises, martial arts, boxing, yoga, bodyweight exercises, etc. I do two at night before I go to bed. What I learned about my body is that when I work out, I work out intensely and get tired afterward. It helps me go to sleep.

Like your sleep experiments, you should experiment with what exercises, time during the day, and duration work best for you.

Exercise: Find Your Peak Routine

Alright, it's time for you to experiment.

For the next 7 days:

1. **Track your sleep.** Write down what time you go to bed when you wake up, and how sharp you feel in the morning (on a scale of 1–10).

2. **Notice patterns.**

3. What's your magic number?

4. Which days did you feel sluggish? Why?

5. Did you eat something that boosted or wrecked your brain?

6. **Write your personal formula.**

7. "I function best on ____ hours of sleep."

8. "My brain loves when I eat ________ for breakfast."

9. "I'm sharpest when I __________ in the morning."

By the end of the week, you'll have your own **brain-fuel playbook.**

One Last Pep Talk

Here's the truth:

You don't have to run yourself into the ground to be a great entrepreneur.

In fact, the sharper you are, the better you'll perform, connect, and lead.

So ditch the "sleep is for the weak" badge of honor.

Start treating your body and brain like the asset they are.

In the next chapter, we'll tackle something equally powerful:

How to eliminate distractions and sharpen your focus.

Because once your brain is rested and fueled, it's time to point it in the right direction.

Final Exercise Recap:

1. Track sleep and mental clarity for 7 days.
2. Identify patterns.
3. Create your personal peak formula.

Chapter Three

Mastering Focus and Beating Distraction

Running three businesses at once sounds impressive when you say it at networking events. People look at you like you must have superpowers.

But here's the truth: behind the scenes, it's a juggling act of deadlines, phone calls, financial spreadsheets, and constant interruptions. It's the entrepreneurial version of spinning plates — except the plates are on fire and occasionally explode.

For years, I thought the only way to survive was to work harder and longer. My days were marathons. I would start at sunrise, plow through emails, calls, meetings, and projects, and look up only when my stomach growled at me around dinnertime. I worked through lunch, skipped breaks, and convinced myself that sleep was optional.

It all worked — until it didn't.

The Cost of Constant Hustle

At first, the adrenaline was enough to keep me moving. I felt productive, even heroic. But slowly, the cracks started showing. I began forgetting little things — people's names, important details from conversations, or why I'd walked into a room in the first place. I'd get to the end of the day and have no idea what I'd actually accomplished. My brain felt like an overworked computer — frozen, buffering, and desperately in need of a reboot.

That's when I realized something had to change. Like many breakthroughs in life, it started with a random discovery and a little experimentation.

The Tomato That Saved My Brain

The Pomodoro Technique.

I still remember the first time I heard about it. I rolled my eyes. It sounded like something you'd order at an Italian restaurant. But after hearing enough people swear by it, I figured I'd give it a shot.

The idea is deceptively simple: you work for a set time — traditionally 25 minutes, but I settled on 45 minutes — and then you take a break, usually 5 to 10 minutes. Then you repeat.

The first time I tried it, I was skeptical. Taking a break every hour? It felt indulgent. But by noon that first day, I was shocked. I wasn't dragging or distracted. I was actually excited to get back to work after each break.

For the first time in years, I ended the day with energy to spare — and, more importantly, a clear memory of what I had accomplished.

One of my favorite tools for this is Pomofocus (www.pomofocus.io). It allows you to set your own Pomodoro time, short and long breaks, and even a list of tasks that should be completed during that sprint.

You can also just set a timer on your cellphone.

Discovering "The One Thing"

Shortly after, I read **The One Thing** by Gary Keller. That book hit me like a freight train. Keller's message is simple: when you prioritize everything, nothing is a priority. But when you zero in on the single most important task each day — your "One Thing" — everything else starts to fall into place.

I realized I'd been spreading myself too thin, chasing too many goals, and measuring success by how long I worked, not how focused I was. It wasn't sustainable. So, I decided to restructure my days around one key principle: do less, better.

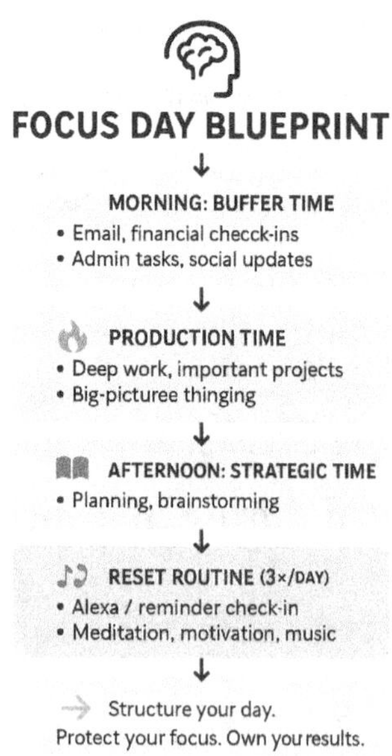

Simplify to Save Brainpower

There's one sneaky memory thief most of us don't even notice: **decision fatigue.**

We make thousands of tiny decisions every day — what to wear, what to eat, when to check email, whether to say yes to that meeting invite. And every one of those choices drains a little of your brain's energy tank.

By the time you get to the "big" decisions — the strategy call, the sales meeting, the creative work — you're often running on fumes.

The good news? You can sidestep decision fatigue by **pre-deciding** and building routines that reduce your mental load.

Here's how I've seen it play out in my own life:

1. On workdays, I rotate similar outfits. It's not quite Mark Zuckerberg's gray T-shirt uniform, but it's close enough.

2. My morning starts with an Alexa routine, so I don't have to decide how to warm up my brain — it just runs.

3. I use a spreadsheet and habit tracker to offload daily decisions like exercise, reading, and admin tasks. They're on autopilot.

4. I batch similar tasks into buffer time — so I'm not switching mental gears all day.

When you **remove trivial choices**, you free up mental bandwidth for what actually matters.

So here's your challenge:

1. Where in your day can you simplify?

2. Can you set up defaults (same breakfast, same work playlist)?

3. Can you batch small tasks into a single block so they stop interrupting your flow?

Remember, your brain has a limited amount of high-quality decision-making each day. Protect it like you would any precious resource.

Designing a Day That Works

To make this work in real life, I divided my day into four zones: Buffer Time, Production Time, Strategic Time, and Learning Time.

1. **Buffer Time** became my catch-all for repetitive tasks — checking emails, reviewing financial accounts, adjusting Amazon store prices, and sending LinkedIn invites. I scheduled it when I knew I'd be distracted anyway, usually first thing in the morning and again later in the afternoon.

2. **Production Time** was sacred. This was when I worked on the big stuff: critical projects, creative work, important writing, or anything that required deep focus. For me, that's usually late morning through early afternoon, about 10 a .m. to 2 p.m. I protected this window fiercely—no calls, texts, or interruptions. If the building wasn't on fire, it could wait.

3. **Strategic time** was when I shifted gears and considered the big picture. I'd use this window to design new systems, plan upcoming projects, or consider the future of the businesses. This

was my space to be creative and visionary without the pressure of deadlines.

4. Finally, there was **Learning Time.** This comes at the end of the day when my creative energy is spent, but my curiosity is still awake. I used this time to read, watch videos, take online courses, or dive into topics that fascinated me.

Alexa, the Assistant I Never Knew I Needed

One of my secret weapons in making all this stick? Alexa.

I set up a routine that kicked off each morning, and I loved it so much that I ran it multiple times a day. It would walk me through my schedule, guide me through a short meditation, play a motivational clip, and cap it off with an energizing song. It was like having a personal assistant, life coach, and DJ all in one.

These little routines became a ritual. They reminded me to pause, breathe, and reset. And as silly as it might sound, those small moments of intention made a huge difference in keeping me focused and grounded, all in less than 10 minutes.

Why Multitasking Is a Memory Killer

Here's something we rarely admit: multitasking is a lie.

We think we're being efficient when we bounce between emails, texts, and meetings. But what's really happening is task-switching — and every time we switch, our brain pays a price.

Research shows that when we switch tasks, our brain needs time to reset. That reset drains energy, reduces accuracy, and makes it harder to retain information. Over time, this constant switching wears down our working memory — the mental scratchpad we use to keep track of what we're doing.

That's why you can't remember what you accomplished at the end of a scattered day. It's not that you didn't do anything — it's that your brain never had time to **focus** and **encode** what you were doing.

The Surprising Power of Rest

One of the biggest myths in entrepreneurship is that success belongs to the person who grinds the hardest. But here's the truth no one tells you: **rest is a force multiplier.**

When you work in focused blocks and then take purposeful breaks, you're not being lazy — you're giving your brain the time it needs to recover and process. Those breaks help clear mental clutter, improve creativity, and strengthen memory.

Once I understood this, I stopped seeing rest as a reward for productivity. I started seeing it as an essential part of it.

Designing Your Ideal Day

So how do you put this into practice?

Start by writing down all the tasks you typically handle in a day. Be honest — include everything, even the mindless stuff like checking social media or reading headlines.

Next, consider when you naturally have the most energy. Are you sharpest in the morning? Do you hit your stride after lunch? Match your high-focus tasks to your peak hours, and reserve the low-focus stuff (like Buffer Time) for when you're more easily distracted.

Then, map out a basic daily flow:

1. Morning → Buffer Time

2. Late Morning to Early Afternoon → Production Time
3. Afternoon → Strategic Time
4. End of Day → Learning Time

Finally, add in a reset routine. It doesn't have to be high-tech. Maybe it's setting a reminder to stretch, breathe, and check in with yourself every few hours. Maybe it's listening to music or stepping outside for fresh air. Whatever works for you — the goal is to interrupt the cycle of burnout before it starts.

The One-Thing Mindset

As you build your new routine, remember: this isn't about cramming more into your day. It's about doing fewer things better.

Every evening, ask yourself: *"What's my One Thing tomorrow?"*

Write it down.

Make it the centerpiece of your day.

That single act of clarity will do more for your focus and memory than any app or hack you can find.

One Last Pep Talk

You don't need to be superhuman to run a successful business—and you definitely don't need to sacrifice your mind in the process. By organizing your day with intention, giving your brain the focus and rest it craves, and ruthlessly protecting your most important work, you set yourself up not just for productivity but also for long-term clarity and sharp memory.

Next up, we're going to explore some of the coolest memory tools and brain-training apps out there — because once your brain is firing on all cylinders, we're going to help you level up even more.

Final Exercise Recap:

1. Write down your daily tasks.
2. Match them to your natural energy highs and lows.
3. Build your own time-blocked day.
4. Set up a reset routine.
5. Identify your One thing for tomorrow.

Chapter Four

The Magic of Mnemonics — Turning Your Brain into a Filing Cabinet

Let's face it — I've been there. I used to struggle with remembering names.

A few years ago, I was at a big business conference where you shake a hundred hands before lunch. Everyone wore nametags, but half the time, they were flipped over or covered by a blazer. By midday, I was running on fumes and vague greetings.

"Hey, buddy!"

"Great to see you again, my friend!"

"Wow, we keep bumping into each other, huh?"

Or, the best one, introducing someone whose name I couldn't remember to another person, hoping that they would introduce themselves and I would learn their name.

By dinner, I was exhausted—not just from networking but also from the mental juggling act of trying (and failing) to remember who was who.

The Bar Conversation That Changed Everything

That evening, I ended up at the hotel bar next to another speaker. We were swapping stories, and I confessed how miserable I was at names.

She smiled and said, "Oh, I use mnemonics for that."

"Mnemonics? Like what we learned in school? Every Good Boy Does Fine?"

"Exactly," she said. "But applied to real life."

She explained how she turned names into funny images, grouped lists into memorable acronyms, and used something called a **memory palace** to store important details.

Admittedly, I was a bit skeptical. But my curiosity got the better of me. So, I retreated to my room, fired up a few YouTube videos, and decided to put it to the test the next day.

My First Experiment

The next morning, it was go-time.

First up: Sarah. I pictured her surfing a massive wave — Sarah the Surfer.

Next: Mike. I imagined him holding a giant microphone, rocking out on stage.

Finally, Jennifer. I saw her juggling jellybeans like a circus star.

Ridiculous? Definitely.

Effective? Shockingly.

Two days later, I still remembered all three names. That seemingly silly exercise did what years of vague 'Hey, buddy!' couldn't. It worked. And it worked well.

Why Mnemonics Work (and Why Your Brain Loves Them)

This works because our brains aren't designed to memorize random data. They're designed to remember **stories, images, and emotions**.

If I give you a list of seven random numbers, you'll probably forget them in minutes. But suppose I tell you a story about seven wild ducks crossing the freeway. In that case, you'll remember it — because your brain loves novelty and surprise.

Mnemonics work because they create mental **hooks.**

When you tie a name or a list to something vivid, funny, or weird, you give your brain something to grab onto. You turn "useless trivia" into "memorable snapshots."

The Tools in Your Mnemonic Toolkit

Let's break down some of the most powerful mnemonic tools — and how to use them.

1. Name Associations

Names are slippery. But if you turn them into something visual or familiar, they stick.

Brian becomes "Brain" — imagine a giant brain floating over his head.

Lucy becomes "Lightbulb Lucy" — glowing with bright ideas.

Tom becomes "Tomcat" — picture him with cat ears.

The trick isn't subtlety — it's ridiculousness. The weirder the image, the more likely you'll remember.

2. Acronyms

Remember ROYGBIV for the colors of the rainbow? Or PEMDAS from math class?

Acronyms are great for lists. Say you need to remember a five-step process:

1. Connect
2. Listen
3. Acknowledge
4. Solve
5. Thank

CLAST. Boom — you just made a sticky memory.

3. Rhymes and Silly Phrases

"Thirty days hath September, April, June, and November..."

"In fourteen hundred ninety-two, Columbus sailed the ocean blue."

We've been using rhymes since we were kids — because they work. If you need to remember a tricky detail, turn it into a silly phrase or rhyme.

4. The Memory Palace (Method of Loci)

This one feels like magic.

Picture your house. Walk through it in your mind. Now, "place" each item you need to remember somewhere inside.

Need to remember a presentation?

1. Introduction → front door.
2. Key point 1 → kitchen table.
3. Key point 2 → sofa.
4. Conclusion → bed.

When it's time to recall, mentally walk through your house. It's like building a playlist in your brain.

5. Chunking

Your brain likes small bites. That's why we remember phone numbers as 123-456-7890, not 1234567890.

Chunking works for lists, numbers, and tasks. Break big things into smaller, manageable pieces.

The last two of these techniques The Memory Palace and Chunking will be the subjects of the next two chapters.

Real-Life Mnemonic Wins

I've used mnemonics to memorize client lists, rehearse speeches, and even prep for podcast interviews.

When I was launching one of my businesses, I had to keep track of dozens of product SKUs. Instead of staring at spreadsheets, I grouped them into categories and created little mental stories around them. It felt silly — but it saved me from constantly flipping through notes.

I once used a memory palace to rehearse a keynote talk. I walked through my imaginary house, hitting each major point in order. I didn't need notes when I took the stage — my brain had already done the heavy lifting.

Humor Is the Secret Ingredient

Let me say this loud and clear: **boring doesn't stick.**

If you want to make your mnemonics powerful, make them weird, funny, and personal.

Picture the client with the handlebar mustache riding a unicycle through your office. Picture your grocery list as a parade of dancing fruit. Trust me, your brain will thank you.

And if you ever catch me smirking during a conversation, it's probably because I've turned your name into some ridiculous mental cartoon.

The Science Behind It All

Here's the cool part: this isn't just a party trick — it's brain science.

Mnemonic techniques help transfer information from **short-term memory** to **long-term memory.** They tap into the brain's natural strengths: pattern recognition, emotional engagement, and visual imagery.

Without mnemonics, "Tom" is just another name in the crowd. With mnemonics, "Tomcat" is a vivid, funny picture your brain can file away and retrieve later.

Entrepreneurs, Meet Your New Secret Weapon

As an entrepreneur, you juggle names, deadlines, pitches, numbers, and strategies every day. Mnemonics give you an edge.

You can:

1. Remember names at networking events.
2. Memorize pitches or presentations.
3. Recall to-do lists or important details.
4. Learn new frameworks faster.

It's like carrying a mental cheat sheet — except it's built right into your brain.

Exercise: Mnemonics in Action

Ready to try it? Let's go.

Step 1: Pick three people you interact with today. They could be coworkers, clients, friends, or even your barista.

Step 2: Make up a vivid image tied to their name.

1. Sarah → surfing.
2. Mike → microphone.
3. Jennifer → juggling jellybeans.

Step 3: Tomorrow, test yourself. Can you recall their names and images? You'll probably surprise yourself.

Bonus Challenge:

Take a grocery or task list and turn it into a memory palace. Walk through your home and "place" each item somewhere. Later, mentally retrace your steps — you'll be amazed at what sticks.

One Last Pep Talk

You don't have to be a memory champion or a mentalist on TV. You just need some simple tools, a sense of humor, and a little practice.

Mnemonics transform your brain from a cluttered junk drawer into an organized, high-efficiency filing cabinet.

Start small. Play with names. Build your memory palace. Have fun with it.

Before long, you'll realize that your brain is capable of much more than you thought.

Next, we're diving into a technique called The Memory Palace. Trust me — you're going to love this.

Final Quick Recap:

1. Use vivid images for names.
2. Build acronyms and rhymes.
3. Practice memory palaces.
4. Make it funny and weird.
5. Try the exercise today.

Next, we're diving into a technique called **The Memory Palace**. Trust me — you're going to love this.

Chapter Five

Memory Palaces — Why "Hat, Fish, Goat" Changed My Brain Forever

Let me take you back in time — freshman year of college, Intro to Psychology 101.

Picture a younger, slightly sleep-deprived Jeff sitting in a giant lecture hall, surrounded by other dazed freshmen clutching their coffee like lifelines. I wasn't sure what to expect that day, but I was pretty sure it would be the usual: a thick textbook, a dry lecture, and maybe, just maybe, a nap if I was strategic about where I sat.

Then the professor — a bodybuilder who had just learned that he was not getting tenure so he wasn't too excited to be there— steps up to the podium and says,

"Today, we're going to build a **memory palace**," the professor announced, his unexpected words cutting through the drowsy atmosphere of the lecture hall.

I perked up. Okay... I'm listening.

Hat. Fish. Goat.

He started walking us through the exercise.

"Close your eyes," he said. "Picture your childhood home. Now, imagine walking through it in your mind. On the doormat, you see... a **hat**."

I'm thinking: a hat? Okay, weird, but sure.

"Next," he said, "look to the right. You see a **fish** flopping on the floor."

Now I'm chuckling a little.

"Then, as you move down the hallway, there's a **goat** chewing on the couch cushion."

By this point, half the class is either smirking or stifling laughter.

Here's the wild part: **thirty-five years later, I still remember those three words — hat, fish, goat.**

I can't remember where I left my sunglasses last week, but those three goofy images are lodged in my brain forever.

That, my friend, is the power of a memory palace.

What's a Memory Palace, Anyway?

The memory palace, also known as the **Method of Loci**, is one of the world's oldest and most powerful memory techniques.

In simple terms, imagine a familiar place — like your house, office, or neighborhood — and mentally "place" the things you want to remember along a path through that space.

When you need to recall the information, you mentally walk through the space, and the images come flooding back.

It's like turning your brain into a giant filing cabinet... except you've got hats, fish, and goats instead of manila folders.

Why It Works (And Why Your Brain Loves It)

Here's why this works like magic:

Our brains are **wired for spatial memory**.

Think about it. You probably remember where you put your keys, the layout of your local grocery store, or how to get from your house to your favorite coffee shop. You don't even think about it — your brain just handles it.

But when it comes to memorizing lists, numbers, or random facts? Not so much.

The memory palace works by hijacking your natural ability to remember **locations** and using it to store other information.

Placing vivid, often ridiculous mental images in familiar places gives your brain a giant sticky note it can't ignore.

Why Stories Stick (and How to Use Them)

Here's something fascinating I discovered on this journey:

The brain doesn't just love **images** — it loves **stories.**

Think about it: you've probably forgotten hundreds of facts you crammed for exams, but you can still recall funny family stories or gripping movie plots from decades ago.

That's because stories activate more of the brain:

1. Visual areas (you're seeing the scene)
2. Emotional centers (you're feeling the experience)
3. Motor circuits (you're imagining action)

When you **wrap facts inside a story**, you make them stickier.

Here's how to apply it:

1. If you're memorizing a presentation, turn the key points into a simple narrative arc.
2. If you're recalling a list, weave it into a short story (even a silly one!) to link the items.
3. If you're building a memory palace, make sure each mental image has action and emotion — turn your "hat, fish, goat" into a scene, not just a

static list.

For example, instead of just imagining "hat, fish, goat," picture yourself **wearing the hat**, **chasing the fish across the floor**, and **being blocked by a stubborn goat at the doorway.** Suddenly, you're not memorizing words — you're living a tiny mental adventure.

Bonus: storytelling isn't just a memory tool for entrepreneurs—it's a business superpower. When you remember and retell meaningful stories, you captivate your audience and anchor your message.

So go ahead — make your memory palace entertaining. Your brain will thank you.

How to Build Your Own Memory Palace

Let's break it down into simple steps.

Step 1: Pick Your Palace

Start with a place you know really well — your home, office, favorite coffee shop, or even a walking route you take every day.

The key is familiarity. You want to be able to walk through this space in your mind without having to think about it.

For me, it was my childhood home. I can still picture the front door, the creaky hallway, the kitchen where my mom made her famous spaghetti — it's all there, frozen in time.

Step 2: Define Your Route

Choose a clear, logical path through your space. For example:

1. Front door → hallway → kitchen → living room → bedroom → backyard.

You want to walk through the same path every time so your brain knows what's coming next.

Step 3: Assign Vivid, Weird Images

Here's where the magic happens.

For each thing you want to remember, create a mental image and "place" it along your route.

For example:

1. Grocery list:
2. Milk → splashing on the front door
3. Bread → balancing on the kitchen counter
4. Eggs → juggling on the coffee table

5. Chicken → dancing in the hallway

The weirder, funnier, or more emotional, the better.

Step 4: Walk Through It

Mentally walk through your palace a couple of times, stopping at each location to see the images.

When you need to recall the information later, just take the same walk in your mind — and boom, there it is.

Real-Life Examples (That Aren't Hat, Fish, Goat)

1. **Client Presentation**
2. Introduction → Front porch
3. Key Point #1 → kitchen counter
4. Key Point #2 → bathroom mirror
5. Conclusion → backyard swing
6. **To-Do List**
7. Send invoice → front door

8. Call supplier → hallway
9. Check LinkedIn → desk
10. Pick up dry cleaning → car in the driveway
11. **Daily Affirmations**
12. "I'm focused" → bathroom mirror
13. "I'm resilient" → office chair
14. "I'm unstoppable" → gym bag

You can build a memory palace for speeches, shopping, routines, or even your kids' soccer schedules.

The Science Backs It Up

The Memory Palace has been around for over **2,000 years**. Ancient Greek and Roman orators used it to memorize long speeches. Memory champions today still use it to memorize decks of cards, strings of numbers, or entire books.

Modern research shows that combining **spatial memory + vivid imagery** activates multiple parts of the brain, making information easier to store and retrieve.

So yes, you're basically hacking your brain like an ancient master.

Why Silly Works

Let's pause on this for a second.

You may be thinking,

"Jeff, do I really need to picture a goat chewing my couch?"

Answer: Absolutely.

Boring images slip away. Silly, exaggerated, emotional images **stick.**

If you walk into your house and picture a loaf of bread... yawn. But if you picture a loaf of bread breakdancing on your kitchen counter? Your brain pays attention.

We're wired to remember what surprises, delights, or shocks us.

My Own "Hat, Fish, Goat" Moment

It's been almost 35 years since that psych lecture, and those three words are still burned into my brain.

But here's the fun part: Over the years, I've built memory palaces for all kinds of things.

I've memorized sales pitches, client names, travel itineraries, and even the order of books on my office shelf.

The memory palace has saved me from countless embarrassing "What was your name again?" moments — and boosted my confidence at networking events and presentations.

And it all started with a professor, a lecture hall, and a goat on a couch.

Exercise: Build Your First Memory Palace

Let's get you started.

1. **Pick a space.** Your home, your office, your gym — anywhere you know well.

2. **Write a short list (5–7 items).** It could be groceries, tasks, presentation points, or random

words.

3. **Assign vivid images.** Make it funny, weird, or emotional.

4. **Walk through it twice.** In your mind, stroll from spot to spot, seeing each image.

5. **Test yourself tomorrow.** Without notes, mentally walk the path and recall your list.

Bonus tip: Once you master this, start adding more locations and lists—your brain palace can expand as big as you want.

One Last Pep Talk

Listen, you don't need to be a memory wizard to pull this off.

You just need:

1. A familiar place

2. A little creativity

3. A sense of humor

The memory palace isn't about perfection but playfulness and practice.

So go ahead: build your palace. Populate it with hats, fish, goats, and whatever else makes you laugh. You might just find yourself remembering things you thought you'd never hold onto.

And years from now, when someone asks how you remember all this stuff, you can smile and say,

"It all started with a hat, a fish, and a goat."

Quick Recap

1. Use a familiar space.
2. Choose a logical route.
3. Place vivid, silly images along the path.
4. Walk through it mentally.
5. Test your recall.

In the next chapter we will focus on the next memory technique called **Chunking.** This technique will allow you to manage tons of data.

Chapter Six

Chunking — How to Outsmart Your Brain (and Never Forget the Chicken Again)

Let me take you back to a day that started with ambition and ended with... chips.

A few years ago, I decided to surprise my wife by doing the grocery shopping. You know, to be a good husband, rack up some bonus points, and show I was a capable, modern man. No list, no reminders, no worries — I had this. After all, how hard could it be?

Well, hard.

Five minutes into the store, standing in front of a wall of produce, I was mumbling under my breath:

"Milk... eggs... chicken... toothpaste... cereal... uh, apples? No... wait, was that bananas?"

As I wandered through the aisles, something strange happened.

A bag of tortilla chips caught my eye.

"Jeff... take us home."

Who was I to resist?

Twenty-five minutes later, I was home, unloading bags and feeling quite proud... until I saw the look on my wife's face.

"Where's the chicken?" she asked.

"Uh... about that..."

Turns out, chips are not an acceptable substitute for chicken. Lesson learned.

The Aha Moment

After that, I knew I had to get better at remembering things — or risk being banned from the grocery store (and possibly the kitchen) forever.

That's when I discovered **chunking**, a brain hack so simple and powerful that it changed everything—not just my shopping game but also my business life.

What Is Chunking, and Why Should You Care?

Chunking is the art of breaking down big, messy piles of information into smaller, meaningful groups — or "chunks."

Instead of trying to remember twelve random items, you remember four groups of three. Instead of recalling a speech word for word, you remember three key sections.

Our brains are naturally wired to handle **small groups**.

Psychologists call this the "magic number 7, plus or minus 2," — meaning most people can hold about 5–9 things in their short-term memory before it all goes poof.

That's why you remember a phone number like 512-555-7842 but can't remember it as 5125557842.

That's why you can remember a shopping list when it's grouped into dairy, produce, meat, and pantry but fall apart when you treat it like one giant blob.

Chunking works because it reduces **cognitive load** — the brain power required to juggle information. When you give your brain an easier job, it rewards you by actually showing up.

Know Your Memory Style: Why Metamemory Matters

Before we go too far down the chunking rabbit hole, let me introduce you to one of the most overlooked but powerful ideas in the memory game: **metamemory.**

Sounds fancy, right? Don't worry, you won't need a lab coat or a PhD for this one.

Metamemory is just a ten-dollar word for **knowing how your own memory works.** It's your awareness of what you remember well, what trips you up, and what strategies actually help you learn and retain information.

When I first started playing with memory techniques, I assumed everybody worked like I did. I'm a visual guy — I love mind maps, color codes, and mental pictures. But over time, I realized something important: not everyone's brain is wired the same way.

Here's what I mean:

1. **Visual learners**: You remember best when you *see* things — diagrams, pictures, color-coding, or spatial layouts.

2. **Auditory learners**: You lock it in when you *hear* it — talking it out, listening to audio, repeating things aloud.

3. **Kinesthetic learners**: You learn by *doing* — writing it down by hand, pacing around while thinking, or using hand gestures.

Once you know your style, you can **choose the right chunking method for YOU.**

Visual learner? Group info into colorful charts or diagrams.

Auditory learner? Read your chunks out loud or record yourself explaining them.

Kinesthetic learner? Jot notes by hand, walk through the ideas physically, or use sticky notes you can move around.

And here's the best part: you don't have to fit yourself into someone else's method. You get to experiment and create your own **memory toolbox** that actually works in your life.

So, as you practice chunking, pay attention:

1. Do you remember better when you draw it?

2. When you talk it through?

3. When you physically engage with it?

That little bit of self-awareness can save you *hours* of wasted time and strengthen your memory game.

Remember: the best memory system is the one you actually use — and the one that fits your brain.

How to Chunk Like a Memory Ninja

Let me walk you through the exact steps I use.

First, group by category.

For groceries: dairy, produce, meat, pantry.

For tasks: morning, midday, afternoon, evening.

Suddenly, you've transformed twelve random things into four simple clusters. Beautiful.

Next, use patterns. This works wonders for numbers. Break down phone numbers, credit card numbers, and account IDs into natural sections. Suddenly, 16 digits don't feel so overwhelming.

Then, break big projects into mini-steps.

Writing a book? Outline → draft → edit → publish.

Planning an event? Venue → speakers → promotion → follow-up.

Managing your day? Buffer time →, production time →, strategy time →, learning time (yep, we're pulling in earlier chapters here!).

And here's my favorite: add humor and weirdness.

Brains love weird. When I chunk my grocery list, I don't just think "dairy, meat, produce." I picture milk break-dancing in the dairy aisle, chicken boxing a steak in the meat section, and lettuce doing yoga poses in produce.

It's silly. That's the point. Silly sticks.

More Everyday Chunking Wins

Once I mastered chunking, I started seeing opportunities everywhere—not just at the grocery store.

Take presentations, for example. Instead of freaking out about memorizing every single word, I learned to anchor myself to just a few key blocks: the introduction to set the tone, three main points to drive it home, and a clear conclusion to land the plane. Suddenly, a 30-minute talk didn't feel like climbing Mount Everest — it felt like crossing three well-marked bridges.

Learning new skills? Same deal. When I picked up the guitar (don't ask how well that went), I didn't try to master everything at once. I broke it into small, manageable parts: chords, strumming patterns, and actual songs. That's when progress clicked, and honestly, it stopped feeling like a slow, painful death for my fingers.

Networking used to drain me, too — trying to remember a dozen names at an event left me sweaty and overwhelmed. But once I started grouping people by table, company, or vibe ("the jokester," "the quiet one," "the big ideas person"), it became easier — and honestly, kind of fun. It's amazing how much less stressful a roomful of strangers feels when you break it down into clusters.

Even planning vacations with my family became smoother. Instead of juggling flights, hotels, activities, and meals all at once, I tackled one group at a time: flights and hotels first, then activities, then food plans. The result? Less chaos and more margaritas.

The magic here is that chunking doesn't just improve your memory — it improves how you **move** through life. You start seeing patterns where before you saw noise, and you realize you can handle more than you thought — just not all at once.

Why Chunking Feels So Good

Here's the best part:

Every time you complete a chunk, your brain releases **dopamine** — the feel-good chemical that says,

"Hey, nice work!"

This creates momentum.

That's why finishing a section of a project feels so satisfying, even if you're not done yet.

It's why knocking out three emails gives you a little high.

Chunking helps you **feel progress**, and progress is addictive in the best possible way.

The Science Says You're Smarter Than You Think

Chunking isn't a "cheat" — it's how expert performers work.

Studies show chess masters, elite athletes, and top memory competitors all chunk information. They don't process each piece individually — they see patterns, and that gives them an edge.

When you chunk:

1. You engage **working memory** more efficiently.
2. You create **meaningful associations** between items.
3. You increase **long-term recall** because your brain has fewer, stronger connections to store.

So no, chunking isn't cutting corners — it's leveling up.

My Chunking Journey: From Grocery Aisles to Boardrooms

After my grocery meltdown, I started applying chunking everywhere.

1. Client meetings → prep, presentation, follow-up.
2. Course creation → outline, slides, delivery.

3. Daily routines → morning admin, midday focus, afternoon strategy, evening recharge.

Not only did my memory improve, but my stress levels dropped.

I felt less overwhelmed and more in control.

And yes, I now nail the grocery run every time. My wife is thrilled, and the chicken comes home safe.

Exercise: Your Chunking Challenge

Ready for your quick win?

1. Make a list of 12 things you need to remember (groceries, to-dos, random words — anything).
2. Group them into 3–4 logical chunks.
3. Visualize each group with a funny or vivid image.
4. Practice recalling them today.
5. Test yourself tomorrow without peeking.

Bonus: Try this at work — break your next project or meeting prep into chunks and notice how much smoother it feels.

Pro Tip: Make It a Habit

Chunking works best when it's automatic.

So start small:

1. Chunk your daily to-do list.

2. Chunk your meeting notes.

3. Chunk your email processing.

The more you do it, the more natural it becomes.

Pretty soon, you won't just be remembering things better — you'll be working smarter and faster, too.

One Last Pep Talk

Look, we've all had "Jeff at the grocery store" moments.

(If you haven't... I'm impressed, but I'm also suspicious.)

The beauty of chunking is that it rescues you from overwhelm, embarrassment, and mental overload — and turns you into the person who always seems one step ahead.

So whether you're shopping for dinner, pitching a client, or tackling your next big project, remember:

Chunk it. Own it. Win the day.

Quick Recap

1. Chunk information into small groups.
2. Use categories, patterns, or mini-steps.
3. Add humor or vivid images.
4. Practice on simple tasks today.
5. Build it into your daily routine.

Next up: How to use and track **daily habits** and amplify you memory like rocket fuel.

Make a Difference with Your Review

Unlock the Power of Generosity

"The best way to find yourself is to lose yourself in the service of others." —Mahatma Gandhi

Hey friend, can I ask you for a tiny favor that could make a BIG difference?

You've just spent time with *Memory Mastery for Entrepreneurs*, learning how to sharpen your mind, boost your focus, and get more done without losing your cool. My goal with this book was simple: make memory tools fun and easy for busy entrepreneurs like you.

But here's the thing — I can't help more people without your help.

Most folks pick up a book because they saw a helpful review. That's where you come in! By leaving a short, honest review, you'll help someone else — maybe another busy business owner, side hustler, or dreamer — decide to jump in and change their life too.

It costs you nothing, takes less than a minute, but it could...

... help one more entrepreneur crush their next big goal.
... help one more business owner stop forgetting names at networking events.
... help one more person find tools that actually *work*.

Just scan the QR code below or click this link to leave your review:
https://www.amazon.com/review/review-your-purchases/?asin=B0DRT8KQJZ

Thank you from the bottom of my heart. If you love helping others, you are *absolutely* my kind of person!

— Jeff Kikel

Chapter Seven

Daily Habits — How to Make Your Brain's Job Easier

I'll let you in on a little secret:

I don't trust my brain.

No, seriously. I love it. It's taken me places and helped me build businesses, solve problems, and craft big ideas. But when it comes to remembering the small, repetitive stuff?

Total disaster.

For years, I ran my life on what I call **mental duct tape** — trying to remember everything without writing it down. I'd wake up determined to be a productivity machine, only to end the day wondering why I hadn't called that client back, paid that bill, or watered the office plant (may it rest in peace).

It wasn't because I was lazy or scatterbrained. It was because I was **using my brain wrong**.

My Spreadsheet Wake-Up Call

The turning point came when I built what I affectionately call my **"brain backup system."**

No, it's not an implant or a chip — it's a humble spreadsheet.

This simple document tracks three key levels:

1. My **daily habits** (things like checking financial accounts, making prospecting calls, staying hydrated, reviewing my goals)

2. My **weekly tasks** (bigger items like client check-ins or reviewing marketing plans)

3. My **quarterly goals** (the big-picture stuff that keeps me moving forward)

Every morning, I open that spreadsheet. It's like a friendly assistant whispering, "Hey Jeff, don't forget to drink water, call Bob, check your Amazon store prices, and oh — take a breath."

Suddenly, my brain was free.

No more mental Post-its floating around. No more mid-afternoon "What was I supposed to do today?" panic. No more skipping over tasks, I *swore* I'd remember.

Later, I experimented with apps like Todoist and Habitica. They're great. But honestly? My spreadsheet is still the heart of the system. It works because it fits me.

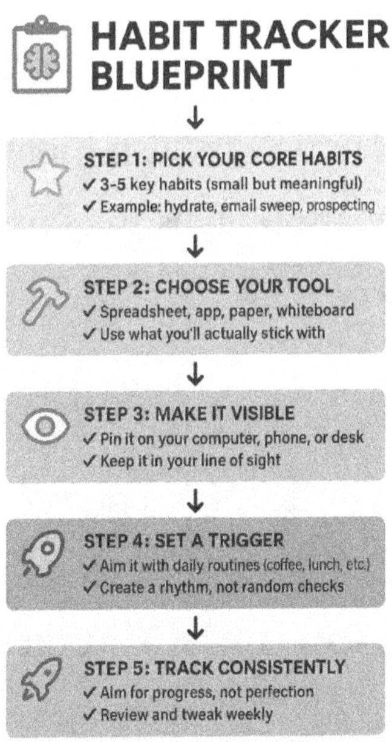

Why Checklists Are Magic for Your Brain

Here's what most entrepreneurs (and, let's be honest, most humans) don't realize:

Our brains were not designed to be hard drives.

We're incredible at creativity, innovation, problem-solving, and connection. But when it comes to remembering to pick up dog food, send that follow-up email, or schedule a dentist appointment?

We're toast.

And science agrees.

Researchers call this **cognitive offloading** — using tools outside our brain (like lists, notes, and reminders) to manage information. This frees up mental space for what really matters.

In other words:

A checklist isn't a crutch. It's a power tool.

The Real Reason This Matters

Let's be honest: forgetting to drink water or send a proposal isn't *just* about missing tasks.

It's about the ripple effect:

1. You feel scattered.
2. You lose trust in yourself.
3. You waste mental energy juggling small stuff instead of crushing big goals.

When you eliminate small tasks, you give your brain room to **breathe** and show up as your best, most focused, most creative self.

How I Set Up My Habit System

Let's break this into a real-world picture, not a sterile productivity outline.

Start small — stay sane

When I first started, I made a rookie mistake: I wanted to track **everything**: my morning routine, workout, hydration, email, calls, marketing tasks, journaling, gratitude, flossing, meditation, dog walking, grocery shopping, deep breathing, you name it.

By the end of day two, I was exhausted — from managing my own checklist.

So I scaled it back.

I focused on 3–5 **core habits**:

1. Hydrate (because you can't think straight when you're shriveled like a raisin)

2. Check financial accounts (because I run businesses, not a lemonade stand)

3. Make prospecting calls (because growth doesn't happen by accident)

4. Send key follow-up emails (because relationships build businesses)

5. Move my body (even if it's just a stretch or walk)

The takeaway? You don't need to track 30 habits. You need to track **what matters**.

Choose a system that fits your brain

Here's the fun part: the tool you use doesn't matter as much as the fact that you use it.

Some people love:

1. Apps like Todoist sync across devices and ping

you with reminders.

2. Habitica, which turns your to-do list into a game with points and rewards.

3. Good old paper — sticky notes, notebooks, or a whiteboard on the fridge.

Me? I'm a spreadsheet guy, and I supplement this with my **Remarkable** tablet. This second tool allows me to track things that are not part of my daily habits. There's something satisfying about opening that file every morning, seeing my day at a glance, and clicking that little checkbox. It's an instant dopamine hit.

Make it visible

Here's where most people stumble. They make a list — then bury it.

If your tracker lives in a drawer or hidden app folder, you won't use it.

Keep it in your line of sight:

1. As a pinned tab on your computer, I use the Chrome browser and programmed my browser to bring up my spreadsheet every day when I

turn on my computer.

2. As a widget on your phone.
3. As a printed checklist taped to your desk.
4. Or, in my case, my Remarkable tablet, where I have my daily calendar and to-do list. I found a website that sells a planner version each year for Remarkable. It is awesome.

Visibility = accountability.

Attach habits to triggers

Here's the magic trick: habits stick better when you **tie them to something you already do**.

For me:

1. I check my spreadsheet with my first cup of coffee.
2. I review weekly tasks on Monday during my first Buffer Time.
3. I plan tomorrow's day before I shut down at night. If not, then I do it when I wake up in the morning at 6am.

That way, the habit system becomes part of my day, not another thing I have to remember.

Funny Failures and Real Lessons

Look, I haven't always been Mr. Organized.

There was the time I confidently told a client their proposal had been sent, only to find it sitting in my drafts two days later.

Or the time I proudly completed all my work tasks... and forgot to pick up dinner on the way home.

Or the year my office plants slowly wilted because "water the plants" never made it onto the list.

The point is that we all mess up. The goal isn't perfection — it's **progress**.

Checklists won't make you flawless, but they will make you **less frazzled and more consistent.**

How Small Habits Compound Into Big Wins

Here's the real kicker.

Habits, when tracked and repeated, create momentum.

You save five minutes here.

You avoid a mistake there.

You reduce stress a little more each day.

Over weeks and months, that adds up to:

1. More done with less effort.
2. More focus on what matters.
3. A brain that feels sharper, calmer, and more under control.

It's like compound interest — not for your money but your mental energy.

The Simple Habit Challenge

Want a quick win?

Try this:

1. Write down 3–5 key habits you want to track.
2. Choose your tracking tool (spreadsheet, app, paper).
3. Pick a **trigger** — when will you check it?

4. Commit for one week. That's it.

5. Reflect. Did it help? What would you tweak?

You don't have to get it perfect. You just have to get started.

My Daily Habit Rhythm (The Behind-the-Scenes Peek)

Since you're reading this, I'll let you peek behind the curtain.

My mornings start with:

1. Hydration (I drink a full bottle of water as soon as I get out of bed – something I learned from Sylvester Stallone)

2. Making My Bed (Ala Admiral William McRaven – If you haven't seen his UT Austin Commencement speech – Google it)

3. Plan out My Day (I get my to-do list together for the day while drinking my coffee)

4. Read something educational (I read to teach

myself something new each day)

I have my **Alexa** programmed for a morning routine that I follow while I am getting dressed.

1. **Review My Calendar**
2. Listen to the **1 minute Market Update** from the **Wall Street Journal**.
3. A **1-minute Gratitude Exercise**
4. A **2-minute Guided Breathing Exercise**
5. An **inspirational clip** is randomly chosen daily from YouTube, a podcast, or the internet.
6. Finally, before I walk out the door, I listen to my **"Wrestling Walkout Music,"** usually "Legendary" by Welshy Arms, the greatest entrepreneur song of all time, or something from Imagine Dragons.

On my way to work:

1. 4-5 Minutes in the car listening to **Fox Business** to give me the gist of what is happening in the markets for that day.

At work, I start my day with a Buffer Session of important but not critical things to start my day from 8-9am:

1. Quickly read the "Market Update" article on **Investors.com** and review the weekly calendar in **Econoday**.

2. Review all of our business and personal financial accounts.

3. Write two book reviews for my review sites.

4. Review pricing in our Amazon store to ensure we are in the buy box.

5. Reach out to 20 or more connections on LinkedIn (preselected on Sunday, so I don't have to think)

6. Review my DM inbox on LinkedIn and respond.

7. Write a unique post, article, or carousel for LinkedIn (part of my 60 in 60 strategy of posting something original every day for 60 days).

One thing of note about the writing portions: I leverage ChatGPT every day to help with my writing tasks. Over the last two years, I have learned to train Chat to write in my style, and it is now virtually indistinguishable from my own writing. This allows me to avoid the "blank screen stare" and focus on getting a draft out as soon as possible that I then go in and edit.

Late mornings (usually around 10 am - 2pm) are spent in **Production Time,** making calls to clients, writing books, working on marketing.

Afternoons are **strategy** and **follow-ups**.

Evenings are **reflection**, **learning**, and a little decompression.

And yes, my spreadsheet holds it all together. I complete each of these tasks every day, and I don't have to think about them. I just follow the checklist and don't clutter my brain.

One Last Pep Talk

If you take one thing away from this chapter, let it be this:

Your brain is too valuable to waste on "don't forget to..."

Set up a system.

Make it visible.

Use it consistently.

Let your brain focus on what it's truly good at.

You were built to create, lead, innovate — not to remember to reorder printer ink.

So build your checklist.

Trust the system.

And go unleash your best, most brilliant self.

Quick Recap

1. Focus on what matters most — start with just a few habits.
2. Use a tool that fits your style.
3. Keep it visible.
4. Tie it to a daily trigger.
5. Commit to one week and adjust as needed.

Next up: we dive into the digital tools that can super

Chapter Eight

Boost Your Brainpower with Digital Tools

Let me tell you about when I was schooled by a grandma named Betty.

It all started during one of those weeks when life as an entrepreneur felt like I was juggling flaming chainsaws. I had six businesses, a mountain of client calls, endless to-dos, and—just for fun—a speaking gig on the weekend. I was running on caffeine and sheer willpower. My brain, however, was waving a little white flag.

At a networking event, while trying to smile through the fog in my head, I chatted with another entrepreneur who casually mentioned she used an app called **MemoryOS** to stay sharp. She swore it helped her remember names, facts, and even presentation points. Intrigued but skeptical (because, hey, I grew up before smartphones were glued to our palms), I decided to check it out. The relief I felt when I discovered these tools was immense, and it empowered me to take control of my mental performance.

That night, I downloaded not just memoryOS but also BrainHQ and Lumosity. And let me tell you — five minutes into Lumosity, I found myself battling it out on a memory game... and promptly losing to "Betty," the app's fictional 70-year-old champion.

Betty, if you're out there — thanks for the humility.

Why Digital Tools Are Brain Gold

I quickly learned that these apps weren't making me smarter—they were making my brain work better *with* me. They didn't replace focus, memory, or good habits but amplified what I already had.

And let's be honest: as entrepreneurs, we need every edge we can get.

We're juggling clients, team meetings, marketing plans, financial goals, and probably a side hustle or two. That's a lot for one brain to manage.

Why not outsource some of the heavy lifting?

Digital Tools That Actually Work

Let's talk about the big three that made my biggest difference.

memoryOS is like building a personal vault for your brain. It's based on the "memory palace" technique, which goes all the way back to the ancient Greeks. You imagine a place you know well — like your childhood home — and mentally place the information you want to remember in different rooms or spots.

For example, if I needed to remember key points for a talk, I'd mentally place each point in a different corner of the house. When it was time to present, I'd just "walk through" the house in my head.

It sounds a little out there, but trust me, it works. And memoryOS guides you through it with easy exercises and a cool virtual platform, so you're not just guessing your way through.

BrainHQ is the brainchild of serious scientists, which is probably why it feels less like a game and more like a workout. The exercises are designed to improve focus, memory, processing speed, and decision-making — basically, everything you need to run a business without melting down.

I especially liked how it tracked progress over time so I could see if I was improving. Spoiler: I was. The sense of accomplishment I felt when I saw my improvement was a powerful motivator. It's motivating to have cold, hard data telling you, "Yep, you're getting sharper."

Lumosity is the fun one. It's a suite of brain games designed to challenge different mental skills, such as memory, flexibility, problem-solving, and speed.

I'd sneak in a few minutes between calls or during coffee breaks, and it felt like a mental refresh. And yeah, maybe I started gunning for Betty on the leaderboard — but hey, we all need a little friendly competition, right?

The Secret Sauce: Consistency

Here's the truth about these tools: they only work if you use them **regularly**.

Think of them like going to the gym. You don't get strong doing one set of push-ups a month. It's the daily reps that make the difference.

I committed to:

1. 5–10 minutes on memoryOS or BrainHQ each morning
2. A couple of Lumosity games during breaks
3. Weekly check-ins to review progress and adjust

That may not sound like much, but it adds up. Over time, I felt sharper in meetings, better at recalling details, and faster at solving problems without adding a single hour to my workday.

Pairing Digital With Daily Life

Here's the best part: brain apps are just one piece of the puzzle.

My brain performance went through the roof when I paired them with healthy sleep, exercise, good nutrition, and daily habits.

For example:

1. **Sleep** → I already knew my "magic number" (6–7 hours), but adding brain training made my mornings feel even clearer.

2. **Exercise** → Getting in a walk or workout before brain training made me noticeably more focused.

3. **Diet** → Staying hydrated and eating real food kept me from crashing halfway through a task.

Think of brain apps like premium fuel — they work best when the rest of the machine is tuned up.

Funny Fails and Lessons Learned

Of course, it wasn't all smooth sailing.

One morning, I got so involved in a Lumosity challenge that I completely forgot to call into a team meeting. My assistant had to text me: "Uh, Jeff... where are you?" Oops.

Or I proudly told a friend I'd set a new personal best on BrainHQ... and she thought I was talking about a marathon. Let's just say I got some odd looks.

You don't have to be perfect — you just have to **keep showing up.**

How to Build Your Digital Brain Toolkit

Here's how to get started without overwhelm:

1. **Pick one memory app** — start with memoryOS, BrainHQ, or Lumosity.
2. **Schedule** a time each day (morning coffee, lunch break, end of day).
3. **Keep it short** — 5–10 minutes is plenty to start.
4. **Track progress** — celebrate small wins; notice how it impacts your work.

5. **Add support tools if needed** — consider task managers (Todoist), note-taking apps (Evernote, Notion), or meditation apps (Calm, Headspace) to build a well-rounded brain toolbox.

Why This Matters for Entrepreneurs

Here's the deal: running a business requires mental stamina.

You're constantly making decisions, switching gears, solving problems, and coming up with ideas. That takes energy — and your brain is your most valuable asset.

Digital tools help you:

1. Stay sharp under pressure
2. Remember what matters
3. Make decisions faster
4. Handle setbacks with more resilience

It's like upgrading your mental operating system — and trust me, once you get a taste of that edge, you won't want to go back.

Quick Exercise: Your Digital Brain Jump-start

Ready for a small, powerful win?

1. **Today**: Download one memory app.
2. **Tomorrow**: Spend 5 minutes testing it.
3. **This week**: Track how you feel — sharper? More focused?
4. **Next week**: Decide if you want to keep it or try another.

Remember: progress, not perfection.

One Last Pep Talk

You don't need to turn yourself into a robot. You don't need to master every app on the market.

But you **do** owe it to yourself to take care of your brain.

Because when your brain is firing on all cylinders, you:

1. Lead better
2. Think clearer

3. Stress less
4. And maybe, just maybe... beat Betty at Lumosity.

So go ahead — give yourself permission to experiment.

Try an app. Build a habit. Sharpen your edge.

Your brain — and your business — will thank you.

Quick Recap

1. Digital tools amplify, not replace, your brainpower.
2. Pick one app and commit to small, daily practice.
3. Combine tools with healthy habits for maximum effect.
4. Track progress, stay playful, and focus on consistency.

Up next: we'll tackle how **stress management** transforms your memory and productivity.

Chapter Nine

Stress Less, Remember More — Why Calm Is Your Brain's Superpower

Let me introduce you to an old friend of mine: Popcorn Brain.

Popcorn Brain showed up a few years ago when I was firing on all cylinders — running multiple businesses, squeezing in back-to-back Zoom meetings, hammering through email, and trying to be a decent husband, friend, and occasional gym-goer. I thought I was crushing it. I mean, it's what we entrepreneurs pride ourselves on — out-hustling, out-grinding, outlasting?

But here's the thing: while my calendar was full, my brain was turning into a jittery mess. I started forgetting things—not just little stuff like where I put my keys, but bigger things like the names of people I had known for years or why I walked into a room.

One day, I sat down at my desk and stared blankly at the screen for ten solid minutes, unable to remember what I was supposed to be doing. It was as if someone had unplugged the Jeff Kikel mainframe.

That was my wake-up call.

I realized I wasn't superhuman — I was stressed. And that stress wasn't just making me feel tired; it was **breaking my brain's ability to work**.

Why Stress Wrecks Your Memory

Here's the science part (don't worry, I'll keep it fun).

When we're under stress, our bodies flood with cortisol. This hormone tells us to run from lions, jump out of the way of oncoming traffic, or panic over that last-minute client request. In short bursts, cortisol is useful.

But when stress becomes chronic — the kind we entrepreneurs often live in — cortisol sticks around. And that's when the real trouble starts. Chronic cortisol exposure shrinks the hippocampus, which, if you remember from Psych 101, is the part of the brain responsible for memory and learning.

So, no matter how many hours you work or how smart you are, your brain will hit the brakes if you're marinating in stress hormones. You'll forget names, lose your train of thought, struggle to make decisions, and — here's the kicker — feel even *more* stressed because you're not performing at your best.

It's a nasty cycle. But here's the good news: you can break it.

My Stress Management Experiment

After my little brain meltdown, I decided to try something radical: managing my stress.

I started small. I learned a basic breathing technique called **box breathing** — inhale for four seconds, hold for four, exhale for four, and hold for four. I'd do it before meetings, when I felt overwhelmed, or when I noticed myself mindlessly opening my email for the fiftieth time that hour.

Then, I added five to ten minutes of short meditations using the **Calm app.** At first, I felt ridiculous — sitting there in silence, trying not to think. My mind raced. My to-do list screamed at me. The cat looked at me like I had lost my mind. But little by little, I noticed something: my brain felt clearer afterward.

Next came **movement breaks**. Instead of hammering through eight hours at my desk, I started taking short walks or stretching between tasks. And lo and behold, I came back sharper.

These small changes didn't just lower my stress — they boosted my productivity and, most importantly, my **memory**. I could finally recall names, details, and ideas without mentally short-circuiting.

It turns out that stress management wasn't just about feeling zen. It was about unlocking my brain's superpower.

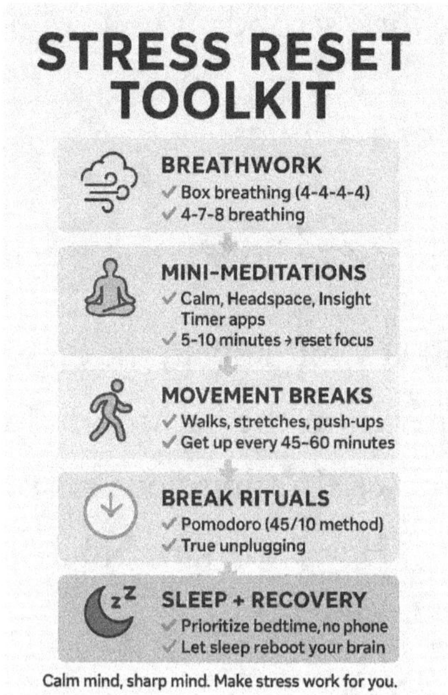

Tools You Can Use to Stress Less

Let's break down some easy tools you can plug into your day to calm the chaos and sharpen your mind.

1. Breathwork

Breathwork is the ultimate quick fix — no equipment required, just you and your lungs.

My favorite is **box breathing**:

1. Inhale for 4 seconds

2. Hold for 4 seconds

3. Exhale for 4 seconds
4. Hold for 4 seconds
5. Repeat for 2–3 minutes

You can do this at your desk, in the car (parked, please), before bed, or even in the bathroom if that's the only place you get peace. It calms your nervous system and tells your brain, "Hey, we're safe. No lions here."

Other options:

1. **4-7-8 breathing** (inhale 4, hold 7, exhale 8)
2. **Diaphragmatic breathing** (big belly breaths)

2. Mini-Meditations

I get it — the word "meditation" can sound intimidating. But you don't need to shave your head, move to the mountains, or sit cross-legged on a rock to benefit.

Apps like **Calm**, **Headspace**, or **Insight Timer** offer guided meditations as short as five minutes. You can do one first thing in the morning, during a lunch break, or right before bed.

Pro tip: If sitting still feels torturous, try a **walking meditation** — just stroll and focus on your steps or breath. It counts!

3. Movement Breaks

No matter how comfortable your office chair claims to be, our bodies weren't designed to sit for ten hours straight.

Try:

1. Walking around the block
2. Stretching at your desk
3. Doing a few squats or push-ups

It's not about exercise intensity; it's about breaking the cycle of stillness, shaking out tension, and resetting your brain.

4. Break Rituals

As we discussed earlier in the book, many people use the **Pomodoro Technique**: 25 minutes of focused work followed by a five-minute break. This technique, named after a tomato-shaped kitchen timer, is a popular time management method that can help you stay focused and productive. I use a modified version: 45 minutes of deep work followed by a ten-minute break.

The trick is using the break well:

1. Don't scroll social media (that's like stress candy)
2. Step away from your screen
3. Breathe, move, hydrate, or just stare out the window

5. Sleep and Recovery

If you've been with me through the earlier chapters, you know I'm a stickler for sleep. Stress and sleep are tightly linked: poor sleep raises stress; stress wrecks sleep.

Protect your sleep like your business depends on it — because it does.

Build Your Stress-Proof Routine

You don't need to overhaul your life overnight. The magic is in **stacking small habits**.

Here's what worked for me:

1. Box breathing before big meetings

2. A 5-minute meditation during lunch
3. A 10-minute walk midafternoon
4. Short stretching breaks between tasks
5. A strict bedtime routine (yes, even entrepreneurs need bedtime)

Stacked together, these micro-habits compound into a calmer, clearer, more focused brain.

Funny (and Humbling) Moments Along the Way

I won't pretend I nailed this from day one.

The first time I tried breathwork, I hyperventilated and made myself dizzy — not recommended. When I started meditating, I lasted all of 90 seconds before itching to check my phone. And walking breaks? Let's say my dog is now convinced I'm home just to be his personal entertainment.

But here's the thing: I kept at it. And over time, I noticed real changes. My brain stopped feeling like a browser with 47 tabs open. I could focus, remember details, and actually finish a thought before moving to the next one.

And you can too.

Exercise: Craft Your Stress Reset Plan

Let's make this real for you.

1. **Choose one tool** (breathwork, meditation, movement, breaks, or sleep)

2. **Pick a trigger** — when will you use it? (before meetings, after lunch, before bed)

3. **Commit to 5–7 days** — nothing crazy, just a week of testing

4. **Reflect** — how did it affect your focus, memory, and stress?

5. **Adjust** — keep what works, toss what doesn't, and maybe add another tool next week

Remember: small wins stack.

One Last Pep Talk

Here's what I want you to hear loud and clear: calm isn't weakness. It's not laziness. It's not optional.

Calm is your **edge**.

When you manage stress, you free up brainpower for the things that really matter—big ideas, creative solutions, clear communication, and smart leadership.

Or, to put it simply:

Your best ideas live on the other side of calm.

So, take a breath. Take a walk. Take five minutes to sit still.

You'll return sharper, stronger, and ready to conquer your day.

Quick Recap

1. Stress fries memory; calm revives it.
2. Use simple tools: breathwork, mini-meditations, movement, breaks, and sleep.
3. Build micro-habits into your day.
4. Small calm practices → big brain gains.

Next, we'll tackle **the power of review and repetition**—the secret sauce for turning what you learn into what you *keep*.

Chapter Ten

Repeat to Remember — The Secret Sauce of Review

Let me tell you about when I thought I would become fluent in Spanish.

A few years back, I was all in. I had the apps, the books, the YouTube channels. I even switched my Netflix settings so I could watch Spanish shows with subtitles — yes, I was that committed. For weeks, I practiced every day. My Duolingo streak was on fire. I was dropping "hola" and "gracias" into casual conversations like a champ.

And then...life happened. Business got busy. Travel picked up. My practice went from every day to once a week to once a month — and then one day, I realized I couldn't remember how to say *"Where's the bathroom?"* without fumbling.

Here's the kicker: it wasn't because I'm bad at languages. It was because I stopped reviewing.

Without repetition, our brains treat even the most exciting information like a guest who overstayed their welcome: they're shown the door, no matter how charming they were at the start.

This isn't just about learning Spanish or memorizing trivia night answers. It is about **how memory works** — and, more importantly, how to make it work for you.

Why We Forget (and Why That's Okay)

Let me introduce you to a not-so-fun brain fact: within 24 hours, you'll forget up to **70%** of what you just learned. This is called the **forgetting curve**, discovered by psychologist Hermann Ebbinghaus.

It's why you can sit through a workshop, feel fired up, and by the next day, barely remember half of it. It's why you can read a business book, highlight half the pages, and struggle to recall even the main idea a week later.

But here's the good news: your brain isn't broken. It's a marvel of efficiency. It only wants to keep what it thinks you'll actually use. So, unless you send your brain the message, *"Hey, this matters!"* — it tosses that info into the mental junk drawer.

How do you tell your brain something matters? **You review it, repeat it, and revisit it.**

My "Ah-Ha" Moment

Once I realized why my Spanish adventure crashed and burned, I started thinking about where else this forgetting curve was sneaking into my life.

Client names? Yep.

Keynote speeches? You bet.

That brilliant idea I had in the shower and forgot by breakfast? Don't even get me started.

I began testing ways to combat the forgetting curve, and I found that the right kind of review isn't just a memory booster; it's a **productivity multiplier**. It helped me sharpen skills faster, recall names and details without scrambling, and—maybe most importantly—build trust with people by remembering the things that matter to them.

So, let's break down how you can use this same magic in your own life.

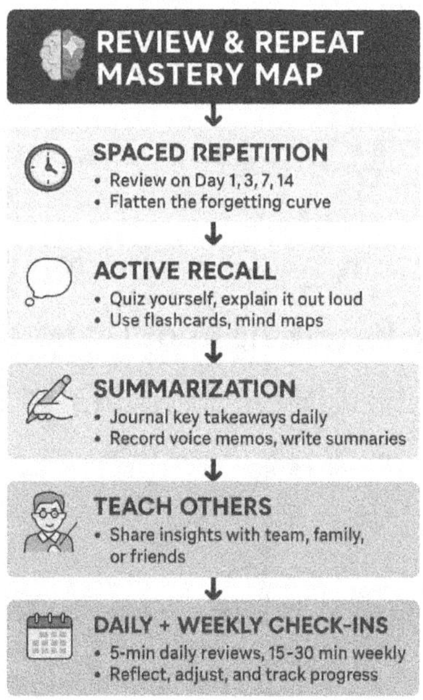

How to Make a Memory Stick

First, let's bust a myth: review doesn't mean mindlessly re-reading your notes or repeating a script like a robot. Effective review is **active** — it forces your brain to retrieve information, play with it, and lock it in.

Here's how to do it:

Spaced Repetition

This is the brain's version of compound interest. Instead of cramming everything into one long session, you space out your review sessions over time.

For example:

1. Day 1 → Review it right after learning.
2. Day 3 → Review again.
3. Day 7 → Review again.
4. Day 14 → Review again.

Every time you review, the "forgetting curve" flattens. Pretty soon, you remember things effortlessly.

I use this trick for client details, keynotes, and even business books. Instead of reading once and shelving the book, I flip back through my notes a few days later and again the next week. It sounds simple—and it is—but it works like magic, and you can do it too.

Active Recall

Instead of passively reviewing, **quiz yourself**.

1. Close the book or app and explain the concept out loud.

2. Teach it to someone else.

3. Jot down everything you remember from memory before looking at your notes.

I don't just re-read the script when I prepare for a speech. I rehearse it out loud, make myself recall key points, and teach the framework to someone on my team. That's what transforms "kinda know it" into "I own this."

Summarization

Ask yourself at the end of each day: *What did I learn today?*

I keep a little journal where I jot down 2 to 3 things I want to remember—maybe a new tactic, client insight, or lesson from a book or podcast.

It's like giving my brain a nightly highlight reel. Summarizing helps move information from short-term to long-term storage.

Teaching Others

Want the ultimate brain hack? Teach.

You force your brain to organize and clarify the information when you explain something to someone else — whether it's a teammate, a peer, or even your spouse over dinner.

I've learned that the more I teach, the more I master. That's why I love writing, podcasting, and speaking—they keep my own learning sharp.

Daily + Weekly Check-Ins

I set aside:

1. 5 minutes daily → quick review of tasks, goals, and important names.

2. 15–30 minutes weekly → Big picture review: What worked this week? What do I want to carry forward?

Without these check-ins, I'd be flying blind. They help me stay aligned, clear, and mentally on point.

Make Review a Habit (Without Losing Your Mind)

Here's where people get stuck: They try to add giant review sessions to already packed days. Don't do that—instead, **layer review into what you're already doing**.

1. While making coffee, recap yesterday's key wins.
2. On a walk, rehearse your elevator pitch or presentation.
3. Before bed, journal your top 3 lessons or takeaways.
4. After a meeting, summarize action items and key points.

It's not about perfection. It's about repetition.

Make Review Work for YOU

Now, here's a little secret most books won't tell you: **review isn't one-size-fits-all.**

Sure, you can follow all the best practices, but if you're using a review style that doesn't match your brain, you're going to feel like you're cramming for a high school test — and that's a fast track to burnout.

This is where knowing your **memory style** (aka, your metamemory) becomes your superpower.

Let's break it down:

1. **Visual learners:** Review with diagrams, charts, mind maps, or even simple color-coded notes. Use sticky notes or digital boards like Trello to visualize progress. Seeing the information laid out helps you retain it.

2. **Auditory learners:** Record voice memos, listen to key ideas on audio, or discuss concepts with a friend or coach. Even reading your notes aloud can help cement the information.

3. **Kinesthetic learners:** Physically engage with the review process. Rewrite notes by hand, walk while reciting key points, or use physical objects like flashcards you can shuffle and touch.

The key here is to **stack the deck in your favor.**

When your review system feels natural, you're far more likely to stick with it—and consistency leads to mastery.

So as you build your review habit, I challenge you to experiment:

1. Test a few approaches.

2. Notice what feels easiest.

3. Pay attention to what actually helps things *stick.*

This isn't about cramming more into your day — it's about working smarter with the brain you've got.

Funny (and Totally Relatable) Moments

Let's be real — this isn't always smooth sailing.

I once tried to memorize a client list the night before a big event. I was up late, drilling names and companies, feeling confident... until I got in the room and called the CEO "buddy." Oof.

The first time I used flashcards, I became so competitive with myself that I stayed up past midnight—only to forget half of it the next morning.

And thanks to my Spanish experiments, my dog now thinks "¡Vamos!" is the command for dinner.

The point? This isn't about getting it perfect. It's about showing up, again and again, and letting your brain do what it does best when you give it the right signals.

Exercise: Build Your Review Plan

Let's turn this into action.

1. **Pick one thing** you want to remember. Maybe it's a client list, a speech, a new skill, or even Spanish vocab.

2. **Set a spaced review schedule.** Day 1, Day 3, Day 7, Day 14.

3. **Choose your method.** Active recall, Summarization, teaching — whatever fits.

4. **Track it.** Use a journal, app, or simple calendar checkmark.

5. **Reflect.** At the end of two weeks, ask: Did I remember more? Did it feel easier?

Spoiler alert: it will.

One Last Pep Talk

Here's the truth: forgetting is normal. But reviewing is your **superpower**.

Repetition doesn't just help you remember — it helps you **master**. It's what separates the people who dabble from the people who dominate.

You don't need a perfect system. You need to show up, repeat, and stay in the game.

Because here's the deal:

What you repeat, you remember. What you remember, you master. And what did you master? That's where the magic happens.

So go ahead — review your wins, repeat your lessons, and let your brain show you what it's capable of.

Quick Recap

1. **Forgetting is natural — reviewing is the antidote.**
2. **Use spaced repetition, active recall, Summarization, and teaching.**
3. **Build micro-review habits into your day.**
4. **Small, consistent effort → big, lasting results.**

The Memory Blueprint — Your Roadmap to a Sharper, Stronger Mind

Well, here we are — at the finish line. And if you've made it this far, give yourself a round of applause (or at least a celebratory fist pump in the air).

You've just completed a crash course in transforming your memory—not with magic tricks or overnight hacks, but with practical tools that are designed to fit into your real life as an entrepreneur, business owner, or everyday human trying to juggle it all. These tools are not just theoretical, they are actionable and can be implemented immediately.

This chapter is your map to pull it all together — so you don't just *read* this book but *live* it.

Why Memory Matters More Than Ever

Before we dive into the summary, let's remind ourselves why we care about all this in the first place.

We live in an age of constant distraction. Our brains are under siege from emails, texts, Slack pings, social media, and the nonstop swirl of work and home life. And yet, the people who stand out today—the ones who lead well, connect deeply and innovate consistently—aren't the ones with the fanciest tech.

They're the ones with the sharpest minds.

Memory isn't just about recalling names or facts. It's about *mental freedom*. It's about clearing out mental clutter so you can focus on what matters, think creatively, solve problems, and show up as your best self.

And the best part? Anyone, including you, can improve their memory. It's not a gift for the few, but a skill that can be honed with practice and dedication. This should give you hope and motivation to continue your journey towards a sharper, stronger mind.

Chapter 1: My Memory Wake-Up Call

We kicked things off with my confession: I've always been great at remembering faces and conversations — but names? Total disaster. I remember this one time at a networking event, I was so focused on making a good impression that I completely blanked on the names of the people I was talking to. It was embarrassing, to say the least.

For years, I leaned on phrases like "Hey, buddy!" or "Good to see you, man!" to cover up my embarrassment. Eventually, I realized I was missing opportunities to build deeper relationships simply because I couldn't recall something as basic as someone's name.

That sparked my journey into memory training — exploring courses, apps, books, and techniques.

Lesson: Memory is a skill, not a fixed trait. With practice, anyone can get better.

Chapter 2: The Brain Fuel Formula — Sleep, Diet, and Exercise

Next, we tackled the foundation: taking care of the *hardware* that runs your memory — your brain.

After a fascinating chat with a sleep researcher on a plane, I shared how I discovered my own sweet spot: 6–7 hours of sleep. More or less, and I was foggy.

We explored how diet (whole, real foods) and exercise (even simple daily movement) prime your brain for peak performance.

Takeaway: Before you blame a "bad memory," check your sleep, food, and movement. A tired, under-fueled brain can't remember anything.

Chapter 3: Focus Days — Structuring Time for Mental Clarity

As a guy running multiple businesses, I used to work in nonstop marathon mode — until I burned out.

Then I discovered the power of structured time: using 45-minute focus sprints (Pomodoro style), separating my day into **buffer time**, **production time**, **strategic**

time, and **learning time**, and using routines (including an Alexa-assisted reset) to stay sharp.

Takeaway: Focus isn't a personality trait — it's a system. When you organize your day to protect your best mental hours, memory and productivity skyrocket.

Chapter 4: Mnemonics — Memory Shortcuts That Stick

We dove into the magic of mnemonics — those fun little memory tricks that help you encode information creatively.

Remember the story I made up about getting roasted at a networking event because I forgot everyone's name? That was the moment I fell in love with mnemonics — using rhymes, acronyms, vivid mental images, and wordplay to make names, lists, and facts unforgettable.

Takeaway: Your brain is wired for stories and images, not dry data. Mnemonics transform boring facts into sticky, memorable anchors.

Chapter 5: The Memory Palace — Unlocking Spatial Memory

Thanks to my intro-to-psychology professor, the **Memory Palace** is one of my all-time favorite tools.

We revisited how visualizing a familiar place (like your home) and mentally "placing" items or ideas along a journey supercharges recall. To this day, I can still remember the goofy sequence from that first exercise: *hat, fish, goat*.

Takeaway: Tap into spatial memory — it's one of the brain's oldest, most powerful systems. Build a Memory Palace to store important lists, ideas, or even speeches.

Chapter 6: Chunking — Breaking Big Things Into Bite-Sized Pieces

We explored how our brains can hold about 4–7 items at once, but if we group those items into **chunks**, we can store much more. It's like mental compression software. For instance, think of a phone number. Instead of trying to remember each digit individually, you can group them into chunks, like the area code and the rest of the number, making it easier to recall.

The story about memorizing 20 random numbers for fun at a dinner party made this one come alive. By grouping numbers into meaningful clumps, I impressed the room. I reminded myself (and now you) that chunking is like mental compression software.

Takeaway: Whether it's phone numbers, tasks, or presentations, break things into smaller, meaningful groups to boost recall.

Chapter 7: Habit Tracking — Offloading Memory to Systems

I love my brain, but I don't trust it to remember everything.

That's why I use **habit trackers**—spreadsheets, checklists, apps—to manage daily tasks, weekly routines, and quarterly goals. Tools like Todoist or even a simple checklist free up mental space so I can focus on big-picture thinking.

Takeaway: Don't waste brainpower on remembering the routine stuff. Build systems that track habits so you can focus on what matters.

Chapter 8: Digital Brain Tools — Technology as Your Memory Ally

We explored the good, the bad, and the brilliant of tech tools like memoryOS, BrainHQ, Lumosity, and old-school note apps. Used wisely, they're like an external brain — extending your memory, organizing your life, and helping you track progress.

Of course, they work best when paired with **offline** practices, like meditation, mnemonics, and movement.

Takeaway: Tech can enhance memory but is no substitute for brain care. Use apps as support, not a crutch.

Chapter 9: Stress Management — Calm Mind, Sharp Memory

Remember when I told you about my Popcorn Brain moment — when I stared blankly at my screen, unable to remember why I sat down? That was stress-wrecking my cognitive function.

We learned that managing stress through breathwork, meditation, movement, and breaks isn't a luxury — it's an essential part of memory mastery.

Takeaway: A calm brain remembers better. Protect your calm with micro-habits that reset your nervous system daily.

Chapter 10: Review and Repeat — The Secret to Mastery

Finally, we tackled the **review** game — the secret sauce most people skip.

I shared my Spanish-learning adventure (and eventual failure) to show why review and repetition are non-negotiable. Whether you're learning a language, prepping for a talk, or mastering a new skill, spaced repetition, active recall, summarization, and teaching others is the difference between dabbling and dominating.

Takeaway: Forgetting is normal; review is your cheat code. Build it into your day, and watch your memory (and mastery) soar.

Your Memory Blueprint: How to Keep It All Alive

Here's your simplified game plan:

Prioritize brain health → Sleep, eat well, move

Organize your day → Focus, buffer, strategic, learning time

Use smart tools → Mnemonics, Memory Palace, chunking

Track your habits → Free up mental space

Use tech wisely → Support, don't replace your brain

Manage stress → Breathe, pause, reset

Review → Spaced repetition, active recall, teaching

Small steps. Big gains. Lifelong change.

Final Words (and a Little Pep Talk)

You don't need a photographic memory. You don't need superpowers. You don't need to be the smartest person in the room.

You need a **system** built on small, consistent practices that compound over time.

What's beautiful about memory is that it rewards attention. The more you work with it, the better it works for you.

So start where you are. Pick one habit. Layer in another next week. Keep stacking.

Because here's the truth:

A sharper memory leads to better business, better relationships, better life.

You're not just building a better brain — you're building a better *you*.

Now go out there, remember boldly, and live fully. You've got this.

What's Next? Let's Keep This Going!

You've made it to the end of Memory Mastery for Entrepreneurs — and that means you're already ahead of 99% of people out there just trying to "wing it" with their brainpower.

But here's the truth: memory, focus, and mental mastery are like muscles — the more you train them, the stronger they get.

So let's keep that momentum rolling.

Here's how we can stay connected:

Download your free Memory Mastery Workbook — packed with exercises, cheat sheets, and templates from this book. Grab it here:

https://businessgrowthproject.co/memory-workbook 708420

Connect with me on social — I share weekly insights, fun experiments, and even a few epic failures (because hey, we're all human).

LinkedIn: www.LinkedIn.com/in/JeffKikel

Website: www.JeffKikel.com

Share this book with a fellow entrepreneur — if someone came to mind while you were reading, send them a copy. Help them level up their memory and focus too.

Thank you for trusting me to be part of your journey. You're not just building a sharper brain — you're building a business and life that works with your brain, not against it.

Here's to your next big win. Let's go!

— Jeff

Enjoyed the Book? Help Others Discover It!

Hey friend — if *Memory Mastery for Entrepreneurs* made you smile, taught you something useful, or gave you a tool you're excited to use, I'd be so grateful if you'd leave a quick review on Amazon.

Your review helps more entrepreneurs, business owners, and everyday superheroes like you find this book and get the help they need.

It only takes a minute — just a few words about what you liked most or how it helped you is perfect!

Leave your review here:
https://www.amazon.com/review/review-your-purchases/?asin=B0DRT8KQJZ

Thank you for being part of this memory mastery journey. You rock!

— Jeff Kikel

Memory Mastery Glossary

Your quick-reference guide to the key terms, tools, and brain hacks we covered.

Alexa Routine: A voice-activated sequence you set up on your Alexa device to automate tasks like reading your schedule, playing music, or running a meditation — basically, your digital butler.

Brain Fuel Formula: A system that combines sleep, diet, exercise, and personal routines to keep your brain sharp and focused. Think of it as high-octane fuel for your mental engine.

Buffer Time: Designated blocks in your day to handle admin tasks like email, finances, and social updates — so they don't hijack your creative time.

Chunking: The art of grouping information into smaller, meaningful pieces to make it easier to remember. Like splitting a long grocery list into "fruits," "veggies," and "snacks" instead of 20 random items.

Decision Fatigue: Mental exhaustion from making too many choices in a day. When your brain gets tired of little decisions, it struggles with the big ones — which is why routines and simplification are your friends.

Digital Brain Toolkit: A set of apps and tools (like Notion, Evernote, or Google Calendar) you use to store, organize, and retrieve important information — so your brain doesn't have to do all the heavy lifting.

Focus Day Blueprint: A structured daily schedule divided into buffer time, production time, strategic time, and learning time — designed to help you protect your best mental energy.

A simple system (app, spreadsheet, or notebook) for tracking daily, weekly, or monthly habits so you can build consistency and momentum.

Memory Palace (Method of Loci): An ancient memory technique where you visualize a familiar place and mentally "store" items along a path, using vivid images to lock in the information.

Metamemory: Your awareness of how your own memory works — what helps you remember, what trips you up, and which tools fit your personal style.

Mnemonic Device: A memory shortcut — like an acronym, rhyme, or vivid image — that helps you remember information more easily. Example: ROYGBIV for the colors of the rainbow.

Personal Formula : Your custom combo of routines, habits, and tools that work best for your brain, business, and lifestyle. There's no one-size-fits-all — this is your recipe for success.

Pomodoro Technique: A time management method where you work in short, focused sprints (usually 25–45 minutes) followed by short breaks. It's like interval training for your brain.

Power Nap: A short nap (10–20 minutes) taken during the day to boost alertness and memory without falling into deep sleep or waking up groggy.

Production Time:Your prime work window for focused, high-value tasks — no meetings, no distractions, just you and your "one thing" for the day.

Review Ritual: A regular routine (weekly or monthly) for reviewing your projects, goals, and memory tools, so you stay sharp and don't let anything fall through the cracks.

Simplification: The practice of reducing unnecessary decisions and streamlining routines so you preserve mental energy for what really matters.

Storytelling as a Memory Tool: The use of vivid, emotional, or funny stories to help remember facts or concepts. Our brains are wired to remember stories far better than isolated details.

Strategic Time: Time set aside for big-picture thinking, planning, and creative brainstorming — where you step back from the daily grind and work on the business, not just in it.

Stress Reset Toolkit: A set of go-to strategies (like breathwork, walking, or music) to calm your mind and reset your focus when stress hits.

Weekly Memory Mastery Checklist: A system for reviewing your week, reflecting on wins, and prepping for what's next — your maintenance plan for a sharp brain.

About the Author

Jeff Kikel is an entrepreneur, author, speaker, and small business champion who knows firsthand what it's like to juggle multiple businesses, endless to-do lists, and a brain that's constantly switching gears.

With over 30 years of experience helping entrepreneurs, professionals, and business owners build wealth, scale their companies, and prepare for retirement, Jeff has made it his mission to help people design not just successful businesses, but successful lives.

What most people don't know? Jeff is also a lifelong student of productivity, focus, and memory. After years of calling everyone "Hey man" at networking events because he couldn't remember names, Jeff dove into the world of memory techniques, brain optimization, and high-performance habits. This book is the culmination of that journey — a fun, practical guide to help fellow entrepreneurs sharpen their minds and thrive in business and life.

When he's not running his businesses, speaking on stage, or writing books, Jeff enjoys cooking with his wife, experimenting with new tools and technologies, and finding ways to turn everyday life into a learning lab. He's also the host of multiple podcasts and the founder of Sure Horizon Retirement Advisors, where he helps clients create stress-free retirement strategies.

To learn more, connect with Jeff, or grab bonus resources from this book, visit: www.JeffKikel.com

Other Books By Jeff Kikel

Stress-Free Retirement Series

10 Critical Mistakes In Retirement Planning (And How To Fix Them)

The Retirement Income Equation: Proven Strategies for A Secure, Flexible, and Prosperous Retirement

Social Security Essentials

Medicare Essentials

Long-Term Care Essentials

Estate Planning Essentials

Identity Theft: The Road To Recovery

Family Finance Series

Family Finance Playbook

Exit Rich...Retire FreeSeries

The Business Owner's Retirement Blueprint

Entrepreneur Superpowers Series

Memory Mastery for Entrepreneurs

See the up-to-date list at: https://www.amazon.com/stores/Jeff-Kikel/author/B017PNDJ16

www.ingramcontent.com/pod-product-compliance
Lightning Source LLC
LaVergne TN
LVHW022216200926
848481LV00006B/1987
* 9 7 9 8 3 4 9 3 5 0 2 9 0 *